Real Life

Real Life

writers from nine countries
illuminate the life
of the modern woman

Doubleday & Company, Inc.
Garden City, New York

Library of Congress Cataloging in Publication Data
Main entry under title: Real life.
"Translated and published simultaneously
in America, Sweden, Germany, Italy, Holland,
Spain, France, England and Israel"
Contents: Introduction by Publishers
Godwin, G. Notes for a story (America)
Arenander, B. The penfriend (Sweden)—[etc.]
1. Women—Fiction.
2. Short stories—Women authors.
PN6120.95.W7R4 1981   808.83'1
ISBN 0-385-15530-1
Library of Congress Catalog Card Number 80-2958

BOOK DESIGN BY BENTE HAMANN

First Edition

CONTENTS

INTRODUCTION

At the invitation of Doubleday, New York, eight publishers met during the Frankfurt Book Fair in October 1979, one each from France, the German Federal Republic, Great Britain, Italy, Sweden, Spain, Israel, and the U.S.A. Their purpose was to discuss publishing projects that might be undertaken in common. Several ideas were put forward. One met with general approval.

At the latest by 1975, the International Women's Year, it became evident that the Women's Liberation Movement was among the decade's most powerful worldwide forces for change. Confronted with divergent national traditions, the struggle for equal rights developed its own method in each country, achieved its own successes, and incurred its own disappointments.

The experience of women in the emancipation process of the seventies has been reflected not only in political developments but in literature as well. To show this, is the purpose of the present anthology. An additional publishing house in Holland has been drawn into the project. Each publishing house has contributed from its own country a story written in the last ten years. These were the only conditions set.

The anthology will appear simultaneously in eight languages and in nine countries in the fall of 1981. It will be presented to the public at the Frankfurt Book Fair in the presence of the authors as the common undertaking of a group of publisher friends.

ALBERT BONNIERS FORLAG, SWEDEN

DOUBLEDAY & COMPANY, INC., NEW YORK

EDITIONS JEAN-CLAUDE LATTÈS, PARIS

EDITORIAL ARGOS VERGARA, BARCELONA

ELSEVIER BOEKERIJ, AMSTERDAM

KETER PUBLISHING HOUSE, JERUSALEM

SIDGWICK & JACKSON, LONDON

SPERLING & KUPFER, MILAN

VERLAG KIEPENHEUER & WITSCH, COLOGNE

NOTES FOR A STORY

Working Title: Childhood Friends

Gail Godwin   John B. Friedman

NOTES FOR A STORY

Working Title: Childhood Friends

by Gail Godwin

A woman, CATHERINE, visiting her childhood friend, NORA. The two have been friends since second grade. Now both are in their mid-thirties. Time of the visit: Thanksgiving, 1973. Place: Woodstock, N.Y. CATHERINE, at this time, is going through a lonely and humiliating phase of her life. NORA, on the other hand, is having her first uneasy bout with security and success.

1 / Two Women

The story might open with Nora walking through the house in Woodstock, going over their friendship, her own life, life in general, etc., while she waits for Catherine's arrival. Catherine telephoned last night to say she had gotten as far as New York and was spending the night with some Yoga people. These past few years, Catherine seems to be running more and more with people on the fringe. Nora, walking through the house—the first real house she has ever lived in—is now remembering how, from early girlhood, both she and Catherine wanted to be writers. They discussed their destiny seriously, as though nothing could possibly interfere.

Nora would go over to Catherine's big red house with the four white columns, and the two girls would lie around in Catherine's splendid bedroom with the door closed, writing stories, while downstairs Catherine's mother wept over some burnt cookies (she was going through the change early) and Catherine's father, a successful surgeon, listened to operas when he was home. Nora would say, "Let's start with the sad whistle of the train today," and both girls would check the clock and write furiously for ten minutes. Nora's heart was in her throat. What if she didn't finish in time? "Time," calls Catherine. Then Nora would read aloud what she had written, and Catherine would read what she had written. From downstairs came the sounds of *Aïda* or *Boris Godunov*, until Nora knew long passages by heart. Nora's stories usually featured a solitary person, a Romantic Outcast. He wandered outside in cold weather, gazing through the lighted windows of big houses, or stood near the tracks and watched the train hurtle by with its low sad whistle. Catherine's stories were social comedies. The train whistle, however sad, was outside the train, while inside, in dining cars or Pullman, the amusing dynamics between human beings went on. She had an ear for dialogue and a knack for getting inside people of all ages.

When Catherine came over to Nora's apartment, Nora always tried to make the room she shared with her mother look as though it were hers alone. Scattered animals around, her books, etc. Hung up things with Scotch tape on the walls. There: an ordinary girl's room. Nora made cookies or brownies. Her mother worked all day. At Nora's they once took the working title "The Magic Lipstick." They agreed their stories should both be about a girl who goes to a dance and has a terrible time until she goes to cry in the Ladies Room, where she meets a beautiful older woman, who says, "Here, try some of my lipstick," and the girl goes back to the dance and is the center of attention. In Nora's story, told from the viewpoint of the young girl, the girl's unhappiness seems to be a permanent state of mind. Therefore the lipstick was truly magic. Anything less than the supernatural would have failed to undo such misery. Catherine told her story from the older woman's point of view. She did lend the girl her lipstick, and they talked. It turns out the reason the girl is unhappy is that she's with a beastly date. The older woman, a chaperone, introduces the girl to her own son, a charming young man, who insists on dancing with her the rest of the evening.

"Catherine has always been so mature," says Catherine's mother in a telephone conversation to Nora's mother. The two women speak dutifully of their daughters, unable to discuss anything else. They move in such different worlds. "No, Catherine was born a young woman," her mother goes on, speaking in a slightly nasal voice, which her daughter inherits. "It's my guess she will marry very young." "How nice," replies Nora's mother, awkward in these conversations because she can never forget that this woman lives in Forest Park and *volunteers* her services to the Community Chest, whereas she herself is the only paid employee. She types the letters, balances the books, runs errands, and makes tea and coffee for these rich women who like to play at working, rushing in and out to show off their new clothes to one another. "Nora is still very much a child," she allows herself to admit ruefully.

Nora, walking around the rooms of the big house in Woodstock, waiting for her friend Catherine to arrive on this sunny Thanksgiving Day, indulges herself in a moment of amazed self-congratulation. "And yet," she says aloud to the warm yellow walls of the room, "and yet, I MADE IT AND SHE DIDN'T."

At about this point, Catherine should drive up in the Volkswagen with her young man. He is extremely handsome but rather ethereal. Pale-red hair, translucent skin, not an ounce of fat. Clear green spiritual eyes. He sits down in the best chair and graciously accepts coffee. He looks round the sun-filled room and says in a gentle drawl, "There are special vibrations in this house." He is going on to Oneonta, to a Yoga residence there, to fast and meditate over the Thanksgiving weekend. He will drive Catherine's car. Then, on Sunday, he will pick Catherine up and they'll drive south again. He is one of Catherine's students at a small Quaker college in Pennsylvania. As soon as he leaves, Catherine bursts into sobs. "I'm cracking up," she says. "I'm being torn apart by the disorganized Byrons in my life and the Astral people. The Byrons sleep with me and run; the Astrals, when they're not flying around in space every night, lecture me on how I should abandon my fleshly lusts."

Nora sits facing her weeping friend and thinks how, for years, she has had the following recurrent nightmare. In this nightmare, Nora is leafing through a *Mademoiselle* magazine, and her heart stops. There is a story by Catherine. That is the whole dream. Nora began having this dream her last year in college, when Catherine was already married and living in Gibraltar with her naval-officer husband, when writing was probably the last thing on her mind. Nora continued to have the dream after she herself had published many stories in national magazines, and several novels. In reality, Catherine has published nothing. She is a professor now and sometimes writes songs, which she sings to her students. She doesn't even want to be a writer anymore. In the dream, Nora has published nothing. The reason it is a nightmare is because of the way she feels while having it: a sick, heavy certainty that she will never be acknowledged. She still has the nightmare from time to time. Often, when she is stuck in a novel or a story, she works the following magic on herself. She pretends that somewhere in the country a person like Catherine is sitting in a room racing her to finish the same story, or that person's version of it. This usually gets her going again. If it doesn't, she "steals" the other person's story: she pretends she is her competitor and writes it from the competitor's point of view.

Have the two women talk a while longer. Have Catherine relate, *in detail*, some of her cataclysmic experiences with lovers. (Catherine has a weakness for younger men; Nora likes the older ones.) Catherine frequently refers to her "constant horniness." Nora disapproves of the term and is a little put off by the thought of this floating lust, or whatever it is. Over the years, Catherine has told some fascinating tales about her adventures. For instance, the time when she was divorced from her Navy husband and getting her Ph.D. at Columbia and living in the Village. Her father, concerned for her welfare, used to send his friends regularly to check on her whenever they were in town. He sent a colleague, a distinguished obstetrician, to look in on her. The obstetrician took her to dinner; then they went back to the Village and she gave him some pot and they went to bed. As a result of the evening, she had one of the first legal abortions in the state of New York. Her father thought he was paying for a set of the Oxford English Dictionary. And the time when an old lover dropped by and they went to bed for old times' sake, and then he asked if he and his new love could use Catherine's apartment when she was away for a weekend. So Catherine went to great trouble cleaning her apartment, stocking it with good food and drink—flowers, too—and while she was putting clean sheets on the bed for them, she *got turned on*. Also the time when she was sleeping with one of her students, a staunch young Quaker, who always got out of bed afterward and asked God to forgive him.

Nora has written several stories based on Catherine's experiences, trying to get inside Catherine and see how such a life would feel. Or she takes Catherine's stories and uses them as anecdotes, scattered about in her novels as conversations overheard in restaurants, etc.

After Catherine has told Nora her latest problems about

the young men who are driving her mad, Nora tells Catherine of an experience she had recently. She has been dying to tell it ever since she knew Catherine was coming. What happened was this: alone in this house, she has discovered a rather dangerous little trick. If she catches herself at a certain point just before she falls asleep, she can get out of her body and wander around the house and meet emanations of herself in the various rooms. These emanations are sometimes the unlikeliest ones imaginable and often she scares herself. For instance, last week she made herself "float" down to the basement, where sat a dikey woman in a WAC uniform who signed her up for a husband. Nora turned slowly to face this husband, having no idea what she would have to face. It was a tiny, shrunken child, neither girl nor boy. "Oh, God!" cries Catherine. "Another Astral friend." She weeps again. Then she becomes very helpful and offers theories about arrested sexuality, possible doubts about one's femininity, fear of loving a man, etc. It is so good to have Catherine here.

"She has known me longer and more intimately than any other person, outside of my family," Nora told her lover, the man with whom she lives, just before he drove away this morning. He said he was sorry he wouldn't be there when Catherine came, but he'd look forward to meeting her tomorrow. Nora's lover, a respected playwright, left his wife and daughter for her. But there are a few tendrils clinging to him from that old life, and he has to go to Boston to have Thanksgiving dinner with them. His daughter, home from college, refuses to visit him in Woodstock. Nora was a little hurt that he chose to desert her for a family occasion, but is also relieved to have Catherine all to herself for a day. "You'll love Catherine," she told her lover (who, to her continued disbelief, seems to have eyes for no one but herself). "In many ways, Catherine and I are the same. We're two sides of a coin. I could have been Catherine, if things had been different; Catherine could have been me, if things had been different."

That night, sleeping badly in the guest room of his wife's house, Nora's lover dreams he is making love to both Nora and Catherine. "Both women were really aspects of you," he is later to tell Nora, after the calamity. To excuse himself? To feel less guilty? "In a way," he will tell Nora, "you set the whole thing up."

Physical description of Nora.

Physical description of Catherine.

After lunch the two women put on walking shoes and go for a hike. As they cut through the fields, Nora is thinking about the way her friend has become a compulsive eater. At lunch: the way she couldn't stop helping herself to more salad, the way she kept picking bits of leftover food from Nora's plate, just reaching across the table, perfectly unaware of herself, and breaking off pieces of cold broccoli and pushing them hurriedly into her mouth. The way she kept sloshing wine into her glass. Compulsive drinking, too. Could it be that she was like that about sex, as well? Is she really about to have a breakdown?

"I am beginning to feel like my old self again," says Catherine. They linger beside the shell of an old stone cottage in the middle of the field. The roof has fallen in, but the stone walls are still firm. Already Catherine has collected (compulsively?) an armload of things: strange dead grasses, dried pods with some cottony stuff bursting out, stiff cornstalks, a few pine cones. Now she exclaims over some loose rocks near the abandoned cottage. She tells Nora that these rocks are probably "special," and they'd better take some home. "I already have plenty of rocks," replies Nora. "Ah," cries her friend mysteriously, "but maybe you need some of these!"

Could it be that Catherine really is cracking up?

On the way back, Nora feels suddenly expansive. The world converges around her in a moment of rightness. She has this house. She has this man. She has this interesting old friend. She has her work. God! It happened, after all. She is no longer lurking on the outskirts watching the trains hurtle by; she is on the train, going somewhere definite, warm and safe and moving. She puts her arm around Catherine, rather amazed at how solid and broad her shoulders are, and says, "I'm so glad you came. We have to stick together. It's people like us who have to make it safe for others like us: *people who go too far*." Catherine hugs her. Nora has the sense of having said just the right thing. Catherine is at this moment seeing herself as "a person who goes too far." She tells Nora this. She says, "What I'm trying to do, ideally, is preserve the fine edge of my madness without destroying myself." For some reason, Nora suddenly feels jealous. Then Catherine says, "I have a confession to make. When I walked into that house this morning and saw that old fireplace, and the books, and the two chairs facing each other—everywhere you looked, things set up for two—I was horribly jealous. But now I don't feel jealous. I feel truly happy. Now I feel I can ask you about your man and not be jealous. What is he like? I can't wait to meet him. How are the two of you together?"

Brief monologue by Nora re "her man." Jake? Edwin? Sebastian? Benjamin? Name should somehow suggest his temperament: volatile but generous; arrogant, sometimes even insulting to friends and equals; indulgent and careful with strangers and inferiors; a few irrationalities left in his character, but on the whole a completed adult; edgy temper; way of fathering things: the way he is always the first to discover the plants need watering; the way he always greets the cat in the morning, benevolently inquiring if he had a good night. As Nora describes ————, the reader should get a sense of the unsaid as well. Like many unsure people, Nora is slightly uneasy about her relationship with ————. Is there something slightly wrong with him to have chosen her, to have upset his life to such a heroic degree simply to live with her? She tells Catherine about the fights they have, exaggerating a little. "You can imagine it. A playwright and a writer. He admits it, too: how a second self stands beside him, directing: 'Now what this scene needs here is an Accusation . . . or a Martyrish Aside.' And I know I have to say the next evil thing that's shaping itself in my head, no matter what happens. I'm already possessed by the words, you see."

"He sounds wonderful," says Catherine. "Your Rudy is clearly one of us."

Get them through rest of day. Quick short scenes, maybe only a paragraph each. Catherine makes quite a pretty arrangement with her dried things for Nora's mantelpiece. She suggests they smoke some dope she brought with her. Nora declines, saying, as always on such occasions, that she doesn't want to "mess up her mind." The rapport between the two cools. Both are embarrassed by it. Catherine sits stroking the cat, who has climbed into her lap. "This is a very special cat," she says in that mystical knowing way her Yoga friend proclaimed the vibrations in this house to be special. Catherine tells how the Yoga boyfriend is trying to persuade her to give up sex. Last night in New York, they all sat cross-legged around a chair and prayed to a pair of bedroom slippers belonging to the Maharishi, she tells Nora. Then the two women have a really good discussion, which Nora can't wait to get down in her journal for fear of forgetting the vital points. Nora is weary. This always happens when she is around anyone, except Rudy, for very long. She feels the urge getting stronger and stronger in herself to get off alone and assess the experience she has just had, so that she can contain it, digest it. Otherwise she will either lose it or be overwhelmed by it. "Would you mind if I went up to my room and took a short nap?" she asks Catherine, who says no. Catherine takes the proofs of Nora's latest novel to the guest room across the hall.

Nora scribbles rapid-fire in her journal.

(. . . But the main thing we agreed on was that it's most important to have new experiences, to let intuition dic-

tate rather than pattern. Patterns = habits. She really
needed to come here. Is being torn in half by the disorganized "Byronic" impulses and the "Astral" desire for
some organizing principle that would redeem her. She
feels no style has yet superseded the Romantic, and yet
we're dying for something more. The next "movement"
may be "an inner movement within each person." Says
the last guys to have said anything pertinent to where
we are were Blake, Lawrence, Freud, and Jung. I asked
why hadn't anyone gone further. She laughed weirdly.
"Because they're scared, maybe," she said. She said it *is
clear* to her that within the next ten years everything
will change: "Our private passions, our way of viewing
our intellectual activities, our concept of 'men and
women,' everything." "Britain is already gone," she said.
"Now our country is going. Soon we'll be controlled by
nations whose histories we don't even understand." I
said, "So are you running out to read the histories of
these nations?" She said in that irritating new "mystical-
mysterious" voice of hers: "No. I think things are going
to be resolved less on a practical level than on an intui-
tive one.")

From the guest room come regular eruptions from Catherine as she reads Nora's proofs. She snorts. She chuckles. She
murmurs, "Hmm?"

Nora wriggles nervously beneath her silk comforter. She
can't stop herself from calling out, "What?" "What are you
laughing at?" "What did you just read?"

Catherine calls back, "Did that really happen that way?"
Or, "I never realized you felt so bad about that." Or, "Devil!
You stole my story about how Gregg recorded hate messages
to me on my tape recorder."

"Are you angry?" calls Nora timidly. Then Catherine begins giggling so frequently that she can't stand it. She goes to

her friend. Who is lying under the patchwork quilt, puffing happily on a handmade cigarette. Nora sniffs the air. "Ah, that's why my book seems so amusing," she says.

Supper. Catherine's compulsive eating. Two bottles of wine. Catherine has brought her guitar and sits cross-legged on the floor and sings a new song she's written about how she wants to be buried beneath an old apple tree, her legs spread slightly apart, to receive her last lover, the earth. Her body sways. Nora suddenly hears the exact nasal intonation of Catherine's mother. She remembers all those cookies. The *Aïda*. The *Boris Godunov*. All of it.

Cut to the next morning, Friday. Phone rings. Nora afraid it's *him*, saying his wife has to have an emergency operation, his daughter has killed herself and he can't come back.

It's Catherine's young man in Oneonta. Her VW broke down completely. A local dealer says either put a new $600 engine in or might as well junk it. Dealer offers a flat $200 for the "junk." Catherine begins weeping, but speaks kindly to the young man, says it's not his fault, etc., she's sorry his retreat is being ruined, etc. They agree to talk later, when Catherine can think properly.

Nora says, "Why don't you call your father and ask him what to do?"

"Are you crazy?" asks Catherine. She weeps some more, then tells Nora how she and that VW went all the way to California and back. She tells about a wild young man in Santa Barbara; a woman hitchhiker in a red cape; a brass bed in a haunted house in a thunderstorm.

The two women wash their hair. Nora borrows Catherine's herbal shampoo. It makes her feel good to use other people's things. As if some of their aura rubs off on her.

Rudy arrives. He's pale and emotional. Had to stop en route for a drink. Saw a horrible thing. Hunters had a huge deer strapped on the back of a Land-Rover. Right in front of him. The dead buck worked itself out of the ropes and splattered to the highway. Rudy swerved, narrowly avoided overturning his car. The animal was a mess.

Physical description of Rudy.

Rudy and Catherine talk. Nora is so nervous she can't listen properly. Will Rudy like her friend? Will Catherine like Rudy?

Rudy steals up behind Nora in the kitchen and kisses her neck. "It seems I've been gone weeks!" he says. Tells her, "Your friend is very nice. But I thought you said you two were alike. Not at all. Does she have Scandinavian background?" Nora is making veal Marsala, asparagus with mock Hollandaise, and a salad. The three of them dine by candlelight. Much wine consumed. Catherine has brought several bottles of Pouilly-Fuissé and apologizes for not being a real connoisseur of wines. "But this is excellent," Rudy says, toasting their guest. It is clear that Catherine finds Rudy attractive.

After dinner everything speeds up, gets blurry. More wine. Catherine shyly brings out an old-fashioned lozenge box with violets on it. She produces a small ceramic pipe, into which she carefully packs some dried herblike stuff from the lozenge box. "You're probably like Nora," she says to Rudy, "and don't want to mess up your mind. But it relaxes me." She lights the pipe and sucks deeply. "I've never tried it," says Rudy pensively, watching Catherine close her eyes and exhale, a trancelike sheen on her face. "But then, until I met Nora, I went around avoiding new experiences." Catherine smiles understandingly, keeping her eyes closed.

Both Rudy and Nora try the pipe. He shrugs. "I don't feel anything."

"Me neither," says Nora.

She and Catherine are dancing together. They sing songs from Girl Scout camp. "Just plant a little watermelon on my grave, let the juice trickle through . . ." "White coral bells upon a slender stalk . . ." "My name is Jan Jansen, I come from Wisconsin . . ."

Rudy says, "Do you have Scandinavian blood?" "No, Dutch," says Catherine.

They all get down on the floor and do Catherine's Yoga exercises. They twist their spines, put their legs behind their heads, squat with their heads between their elbows. "I feel the blood in my eyes," says Rudy. "Perhaps that's enough for now."

Rudy has an arm around both women. "One dark and one fair," he says, delightedly looking from one to the other.

The lights are off. They are lying on a fur blanket in front of the blazing fire. Nora is writhing about in someone's embrace. Someone kisses her very softly on the mouth. Rudy is talking to Catherine in a teasing voice. Catherine laughs. Her breasts are somehow bare. She is taking down her tights when Rudy explains in a cordial voice that it's only proper that he be with Nora first. Catherine says, "Of course." Nora closes her eyes. Someone is expertly removing her jeans, then her panties. Now they are rubbing her. She puts her hands over her eyes and says, "No, you two go first. I don't mind, I don't mind. . . ."

Rudy and Nora in their bedroom. "It's all right, it's all right," he is saying. "Nothing happened. Thank God. What brought me to my senses was seeing you lying there, those poor little bare legs, with your fingers over your eyes, and that sad little voice saying, 'I don't mind, I don't mind, I don't mind. . . .'"

Nora thinks he ought to go down and comfort Catherine. "Her life lately has been one long stream of rejections." So Rudy goes down. He comes back and says, "She's fine. We sat and talked. I rubbed her back. She was fully dressed. She said she wants to stay down with the fire for a while and read the proofs of your book."

Later, Rudy was to say: "It was a bit much. First two women wanted me, then neither of them would have me. It was she who took off your jeans and your panties, you know."

III / The Couple and the Woman

First thing next morning, Saturday, Nora makes herself go to Catherine and say, "I'm sorry about last night." She expects Catherine to be cool, stand-offish, but Catherine puts her arm around Nora and says warmly, "Don't worry! You two just weren't ready yet." Once Nora and Catherine were captains of rival teams at the grammar school. They agreed to split their prize, whichever team won. Nora's did. The prize was a white yo-yo with a purple stone in it. Nora can still see the young Catherine, blond hair streaming from the open window of her father's Lincoln, as she calls cheerfully to Nora, who is walking home alone with her prize, "It's okay! Everyone knows you can't split a yo-yo!" The sleek black car gathers speed and disappears through the gates of the school.

What to do about Catherine's VW? Should Rudy drive them to Oneonta so Catherine can at least say goodbye to her car? He looks tired this morning, but seems willing. Catherine is the one who must be looked after today, he and Nora have agreed. They look up Oneonta on the map. Too far for a sentimental journey. Should she take the $200 or put in a new engine? Nora says, "Please, *please* call your father." Catherine: "Look, I haven't been struggling free of all that for years to call him now." But Nora wears her down. While Catherine speaks long distance to her father, Nora sits beaming, her eyes bright. She can just picture him—older now, of course—the everlasting pipe clenched in the prominent jaw, so pleased that his daughter still consults him. "What are you so happy about?" Rudy asks, smiling with puzzlement.

Catherine telephones young man in Oneonta. Says junk the car. She'll take bus and meet him in New York tomorrow and they'll rent car to drive back to school. "My father's giving me one of his," Nora hears her say with a sigh. "He always hated my having VWs and was rather pleased about the whole thing."

Catherine's last evening. Whispered consultation between Nora and Rudy. *No smoking tonight.* Calm, civilized evening. Good food, modest amount of wine, send her away with good memories. Rudy builds a nice fire. Catherine, wearing long quilted skirt, lies on the floor. She is trying to finish Nora's new book. Nora is particularly anxious for her opinion and gets annoyed when Rudy keeps interrupting her with questions. "What do you think of Nora's book?" he asks. "It must be interesting for you, set in the place where you both grew up." Catherine says, "I think she'll get attention for this book. Yes, it is fun for me to see how these things looked from her side."

"They looked different from your side?" Nora asks, pouring herself more wine.

The two friends get into an involved discussion of their youth, the town, the way Catherine saw things, the way Catherine thought Nora saw things, etc. What must come out here is Nora's realization that her *best and oldest friend* never knew that she, Nora, suffered. The more Catherine tells her how "I always thought you were a congenitally private person," the more loudly Nora protests, "No, no . . . that was a front." They forget the time. They forget where they are. Their voices become high, like little girls. It is as though they are back in Catherine's bedroom, revealing their true selves at last. Have Nora become conscious of how much she withheld in those days. Even in those stories they wrote, how she had been careful to conceal, behind the per-

sona of that sexless Solitary who stood aloofly apart, her envy
and her longing to have Catherine's easier way of being in
the world, calling sportingly from her father's car, "Can't
split a yo-yo!" How lightly she had ridden away from her
losses! Had winning meant little to her as well? Is this why
she was able to lend her apartment to other lovers, and let
young men drive away her cars and lose them, and pass it off
with cheerful gallantry when, in front of a fire, a potential
lover suddenly desists for the sake of someone else? Is this
why she found it unnecessary to become a writer: she just
didn't have that many scores to settle? "I had no idea you felt
that way," Catherine keeps repeating. Nora, feeling that she
can at last be herself, that her accomplishment allows her,
says: "If you knew how I wanted to make my début with
you!" "How odd!" cries Catherine. "I remember how caustic
you were about it. The day we met downtown and you
wouldn't come with me to fit my dress. I cried the rest of
that day. I considered not going through with it. You convinced me the whole thing was so shallow." More such reve-
lations on both sides.

Suddenly they smell burnt hamburger. Nora rushes to the
kitchen. "But what are you doing?" she says to Rudy, who
stands rather petulantly over the frying pan, the flame on too
high. Her good copper-bottom pan, too. "We're having steak
for supper!" she cries. He says he can't wait all night to eat,
etc.; it's already ten o'clock. Nora realizes he resents them for
leaving him out for so long. He takes his burnt hamburger to
the table and begins eating it. She flies into a rage and tells
him he has ruined Catherine's last night. The two begin
shouting at each other. Catherine rushes in and tries to make
peace. She takes the steaks out and begins to season them.
"Come on, you two!" Nora goes upstairs in a fury, calling
back she wants no dinner. She bolts herself into the bedroom
and for some reason (the wine, perhaps?) goes into the closet
and sits on the floor. She hears them come after her. "Nora,
please," Catherine calls, rather amused, through the door,

"let's all make up and have dinner." "I'm not mad anymore," calls Rudy. Nora hugs her knees in the closet. Hears them consult in lowered voices. "Better let it be," says Rudy. "No, it's childish," says Catherine. "Nora?" she calls, "Nora, listen: if you don't come out right now, Rudy and I are going to screw right in front of this door." Rudy says, "No, no, that's not the tactic to take, Catherine. You go on down." Then he calls through the door, "Nora? We all drank too much. Please. Come down and let's have our steak and go to bed. I'm very tired."

The three at dining-room table. Somehow, dinner has gotten made by someone. They are having an animated discussion about risk-taking vs. security. Catherine, very drunk, is declaiming about the necessity of taking chances in order to "stay alive." She is treating her hosts rather like small children who have quarreled and been foolish and now must submit to a lecture on the responsibilities of life. She tells them that artists especially must court the unseemly, look violence and change in the face, or their art will become hermetic and dead. "I abhor violence," says Nora suddenly. "I don't want it in my life or in my art. The security I've had here in this house has allowed my work to blossom." Rudy is moved. Puts his hand over Nora's. "There is too much worship of violence for its own sake," he says gently to Catherine. "As for change, that, too, can become overvalued. We are too much a nation of fads as it is." Nora is thinking of his fury over a certain sentence in the *Times* about his last play. Catherine reaches across the table, picks green beans first from Rudy's plate, then from Nora's. She seems unaware she is doing this. She hums under her breath. When she has picked everything off their plates, she shakes salt into her hand and eats it from her fingers. Rudy pours the last of the wine from that bottle. His face looks drained. He excuses himself and says he'll turn in early, if the women will forgive him.

Catherine and Nora washing and drying the dishes. Catherine, very agitated, pursues the subject of violence and change and risk. Nora gives short, noncommittal answers, wanting to go to bed herself. Catherine says, "The trouble with you, Nora, is that you are not a person who goes too far, like you said on the walk. You are only a voyeur of people who go too far. You like to hear about my risks, but you curl up like a hothouse lily if anyone asks you to share them."

"If you mean about last night," says Nora, "I just don't go in for group sex." She rewipes a wineglass that Catherine has dried carelessly. "What's wrong with *sharing?*" asks Catherine. "He loves you. There's enough love there. It wouldn't have depleted his store of love for you. He loved the idea of our friendship, too. And there is love between you and me, whether you'll admit it or not. Last night could have been beautiful if you had let it. It wouldn't have diminished you *or* your precious art."

"It would have been demeaning," Nora replies curtly.

"Demean?" Catherine says in a strange, hushed voice. "Demean? What is demean?" She shakes her head from side to side. Her eyes look glazed, like a zombie's. "Demean is just a word in the dictionary," Catherine says. "I'm more important than the damn dictionary."

Here it must be made clear that Nora sees that her friend has gone out of control and that the best thing to do would be agree with her. ("Of *course* you are more important than the dictionary, Catherine.") But, at the same time, she is looking at this raving, glassy-eyed woman, her chin thrust aggressively into Nora's face. Just like a prizefighter, Nora is thinking, a strident aggressive person. How could I ever have thought her beautiful? At the same time, certain irresistible words are forming themselves into a sentence in her head. Exactly as they do in her fights with Rudy, the fights she was telling Catherine about yesterday. The words are "The dictionary is all we have," and she, of course, must say them. With a wicked calm.

A few seconds later, she has fled outside, into the freezing night. She is crouched behind a pile of rocks, her cat shivering beside her, as they listen to the smashing of glassware, the splintering of wood, dishes being thrown against the walls. And a woman's voice shrieking, over and over: "The *dic*tionary! The *dic*-tionary! Oh, my God, the goddamned dictionary! I'll tear this fucking house apart, you fucking coward bitch!" Then hurried footsteps on the stairs. The deep, angry voice of a man: "Stop that. Stop that. Come to your senses or I'll have to hit you."

"Hit me! KILL me!" comes the banshee shriek.

Give atmosphere of utter silence. No sounds from the house. The close, clear stars, winking impersonally from the cold sky. The calm impersonality of the Solitary, alone in the night with a black cat, gazing toward the lighted windows of a big house . . .

Later he is to say: "The strength of that girl was phenomenal. I had to use the full force of my body to hold her down. That is when my dressing gown came open. That is when I saw there was nothing . . . nothing. She was lying under me with her skirt around her waist, and I hadn't the least urge . . . not the least." He repeats this afterward many times. It seems important to him. Once he adds: "I was relieved to find that out about myself. I have often been afraid . . . certain people are aroused by sadistic opportunities . . . but, no, I hadn't the least urge. At that moment she wasn't even a woman to me. And I think she knew it, and because of this I was able to calm her. We would have talked awhile and all gone to sleep, if you hadn't come in and started everything over."

When Nora returns to the house, she is obsessed with only one thing: tidying up the mess. The cat refuses to come in with her. Nora single-mindedly edits out the sound of their voices coming from the living room. She sweeps broken glass into one pile . . . broken dishes into another. She must put her house in order. That is the only task in the world she cares about.

Rudy calls from the living room, rather apologetically: "Er, Nora, could you come in here for a moment? Catherine would like it if we all talked for a few moments. Please. You can sweep later." Nora goes to the living room, still carrying her broom. The two of them are sitting cross-legged on the floor, near to the fire, which has died. Catherine is explaining, in the singsongy-preachy tone she used on them at dinner, that all she wants from life is for people to share. She is willing to share everything: if the rest of the world was the same, there would be no war, no poverty, no loneliness. Her body is swaying. She has another glass of wine now, and as she sways with it some of it slops over the edge of the glass and onto the carpet, just missing Nora's proofs. "Yes, yes," Rudy is saying, humoring her like a child or a dangerous inmate. "Nora," he says, "do come and sit here with Catherine and me. That's all she wants. For us all to be friends. Then we can go to bed."

Nora stands looking down at them. She leans on her broom.

"Please, come sit with us in a circle," says Catherine. This time her wine makes a tiny splatter at the edge of Nora's proofs. Nora swoops down and rescues them. Holding them tightly in one arm, balancing on her broom, she feels the fatal, fully formed sentence rising in her throat. "I refuse to sit down on the floor, in a *circle*, with a goddamn middle-aged hippie who has wrecked my home," she says.

How are fights, real physical fights, described in fiction? Movies much better medium to get action across, the slow angelic flight of a body through the air, the clean crack of bone against bone. In the less sophisticated plays, Rudy says, a wooden clapper is still used to simulate a fist hitting a jaw. Are fights to the finish different in quality when they are between women instead of men?

"THE SLOW ANGELIC FLIGHT OF A BODY THROUGH THE AIR."
Nora is mesmerized by these words. For months after, she
has only to think them softly and the entire scene comes
back. How, effortlessly, as in a dream, her own slender arm
reached out and gracefully wound Catherine's long light hair
in a secure coil round her own wrist. The simple snapping
action of that wrist, with a strength in the arm that must
have lain unused for years, like so many of her other hidden
powers, which were now, in this atmosphere of security,
revealing themselves for the first time. How had she done
it? The miracle of Catherine, not a slender woman, floating
light as a thistle in that momentary arc of night air. For,
somehow, they were all outside. Rudy, in his green silk dressing gown and the old pair of bedroom slippers. He calls
something to them urgently, but neither can hear him. Catherine in the long quilted skirt and torn blouse . . . the skirt
swirled gracefully
billowed elegantly?
wafted gently?
in its own trajectory as Catherine's head floated down, toward the rock.

("I already have plenty of rocks," replies Nora. "Ah, but
maybe you need some of these!" cries her friend mysteriously.)

Two women. Two women and a man. A couple and a
woman. Three civilized people. An intellectual and two artists. A professor of English at a small Quaker college. A respected playwright who, according to a *Times* critic, "still
labors, albeit brilliantly at times, under the medieval assump-
tion that morality can be legislated by the dramatist." A not
unknown novelist who writes mostly about the Person of
Sensitivity who, by his sensibilities and stubborn sense of self,
manages to transcend the miseries and deprivations of childhood.

IV / The Women

Nora's journal.

Tues., Nov. 27—On Sunday morning, at app. 2:30 A.M., the troopers and the ambulance left. Rudy left yesterday for New Haven. Long Wharf may do *Thieves' Honor* next spring. On Sunday we stayed in bed all day, with the door locked and the shades down, trying to assimilate It in order that It might not swallow us. We made tea for each other. I got up after dark and vacuumed up the rest of the glass. We put the broken chair in the garage. We had already flushed the pot down the toilet. We kept finding dried blood everywhere, a drop even on the lampshade. (?) Rudy dreamed we were in a Land-Rover and her carcass was tied to the back—just like that deer's—and it kept falling off, onto the road. I nursed my arm, fearing gangrene. How long will her teeth marks be on my left arm? A perfect bite. She had the best orthodontist in town. I keep remembering (with something fearfully akin to pleasure) how I grabbed her so effortlessly by her own hair and whipped her to the ground. It will be a long time before I forget the sight of her face as she sat astride me, the ashtray lifted over her head. The last words she said to me as she left with the troopers were: "And, Nora, I hope you keep your precious sensitivity." A very shocking thing happened. At one point Rudy broke down and sobbed like a baby. I have never seen a man cry. Catherine brought back the entire experience with his sister. When she came to live with him after she got out of the asylum. How she attacked him with a knife and he couldn't handle it and called the asylum people to come and get her. Just as he called the town rescue squad when we got too much for him the other night. He sobbed and sobbed. He still blames himself for his sister's suicide in the asylum. We lay around scaring each other about how much worse it could have been.

N: "If her head had hit the rock . . ."

R: "Her head was nowhere near the rock."

R: "If I hadn't had the quick instinct to put that little tin of marijuana in my pocket when I did. I just walked past the trooper, my heart in my throat, and slipped it casually into my dressing gown. . . ."

N: "We would have made headlines in the *Enquirer* . . ."

R: "PLAYWRIGHT'S WOODSTOCK HAREM: SEX, SIN, POT . . ."

N: "The one thing I'll never be able to forget from this whole thing is how easy it would be to kill someone . . . that light, carefree sensation . . . the joyful disposal of an encumbrance. I know now that I am a person capable of killing."

R: "Oh, come. You're being too hard on yourself, as usual. Well, one thing for sure. She had her way. She made us look violence in the face."

Wed., Nov. 28—She just phoned. We talked for an hour on her money; then I called her back and we talked for another hour on mine. She said she "blanked" from just after the time she came up to plead with me to open the door before dinner till the time she and the woman from the rescue squad were kneeling together on the floor and the woman was asking her if she'd ever been in a mental hospital before. Said she snapped to her senses. "I imagined myself calling the chairman at my college, telling him I was in a mental hospital and couldn't meet my classes on Monday. . . ." Said she also called to apologize if she had destroyed anything. Said when she discovered bruises all over her body and cuts on her hands and feet she wondered if she had been violent with anyone. Her theory: that we had all three, somewhere in ourselves, made a pact to have a witches' sabbath. She said what had made her so angry with me was my assurance that I

could have my safe, well-ordered life *and* my interesting demons in the basement. She hates for people like me not to
come up from underground and be counted. The troopers
took her to a hunters' lodge in Saugerties and then to the bus
station next morning. They told the man at the desk there'd
been a drunken party at some playwright's house and we all
went mad. One of the troopers was interested in her. "If I
had given him the least sign, I could have made him come
back later, but I thought I'd done enough for one night."
Said she hoped we could be friends again. Said she didn't entirely discount what I'd said about conserving your energies
for the things you wanted to do most, since she had been
bringing catastrophes on herself with some regularity lately.
Said she might see a psychiatrist. Said Sunday in New York
she just sat around the yogi's apartment and meditated on her
lack of spiritual progress. "There was an analyst in the same
room; he'd been through a Jungian analysis himself, but it
was Sunday and he was playing with his kid and I didn't
want to dump that on him." All the way back to the Quaker
college, she said, the young man had played a tape deck of
his horoscope in the rented car.

We both agreed to write up accounts of what happened
that night and exchange them.

> The pattern: the united couple disrupted by outside
> force. In most Gothic fiction the innocent comes to the
> house of the dark forces. In this case the dark force (dis-
> guised as the fair heroine) will come to the house of the
> innocents.
>
> Dilemma: can the couple who have fought so hard for
> their work and love feel justified in sacrificing the dark
> force without murdering a part of themselves?
>
> How could they have assimilated her?
>
> Explanation: breakup of the conscious status quo by
> influx of new energies from the unconscious.

I told her how we had been so upset by it that we had spent most of the day holding on to each other. She began to cry softly and said, "I had nobody to hold on to."

V / The Couple

It is the following spring. Rudy and Nora walk in the fields. She can't get started on anything new. He is in the middle of a play based on the life of his sister. They pass the ruined stone cottage. Someone is rebuilding it from the inside. It has a new shingled roof. A perfect situation for some artist with limited means and a large need for privacy. Nora says, "I tried again today to write about the Catherine Thing (their name for it now), but it didn't get anywhere. I couldn't decide on a beginning or an end. I do wish she had kept her promise and sent her side of it, but she said she got busy with school and then she fell in love with the new religion professor."

"Oh, yes, how is that going?" asks Rudy.

"It's not, unfortunately. He's had to fight against homosexual tendencies for years, and he says because of her rampant aggressiveness she's almost pushed him over the edge. His psychiatrist told him not to see her anymore. He's very nasty to her at school, and one day she got so paranoid about it she stayed home. She says she still loves him. She loves the potential shape of all he was meant to be."

They walk awhile, without speaking. Describe fields, springtime, nature, etc. Nora says: "I couldn't decide how the story should end. First I thought, Let her head hit the rock. But then I thought, No, that way she would win: she would have brought violence into my art as well as my life. Also, violent endings are so easy. They spare the characters the necessity of coming to terms with all the disturbing loose ends. Also, I had already killed Catherine once in a story I wrote when we were sixteen. I had her and her boyfriend go over the edge of a mountain in his car. It was a sad story. It was told from the friend's point of view. I called it 'Friends and Lovers.' The boy's name was Derwent. I had dated him first, but he fell in love with Catherine and they went steady all during high school. It was because of him that she rushed through college, did four years in three, so that they could get married. In the end, she married someone else, however."

Rudy says, "Your friend is certainly a mixed-up girl."

The following November, Rudy and Nora go to great trouble to find a Thanksgiving card for Catherine. They finally choose a Dutch interior with a bowl of fruit on the table by a window. Rudy writes in the card, "We hope someday you will come and see us again." "We really mean it," adds Nora. And they did mean it.

On the days when she is alone in the house, Nora shampoos her hair in the herbal shampoo Catherine used. She puts on a black leotard just like Catherine's and does the Yoga exercises from a book recommended by Catherine. These rituals have a magic calming power on her soul, which is still troubled by having found love and success after all.

THE PENFRIEND

("Brevvännen")

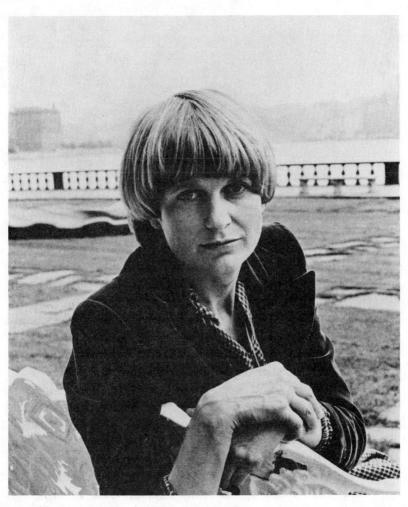

Britt Arenander

BRITT ARENANDER, *born in Stockholm in 1941, B.A. 1967. Has worked as a journalist, social worker, and secretary. Most recent post in the secretariat of the Swedish section of Amnesty International. Worked for the last two years purely as a freelancer. Translates literary works from French and English; among other things, has translated four parts of Anaïs Nin's Diary. Occasionally writes literary criticism, film reviews, and articles on subjects of debate.*

*Britt Arenander is also one of the foremost names in a new generation of Swedish authors. She has published several novels—*The Step, *1968;* Off, *1969;* All Bridges Burnt, *1971;* All There Is to Get, *1976;* Your Own Map, *1979—and a collection of poems,* Dreams of the Reality Outside Stockholm, *1974.*

Of herself Britt Arenander says: "Am divorced, have a fifteen-year-old son and a large blue-gray cat. Have lived for a number of years with a sculptor. He is not interested in literature, and I am not interested in art. My son only reads Donald Duck *and thrillers.*

"At the moment I'm busy translating the fifth part of Anaïs Nin's Diary, and sometimes I write the odd poem or two."

THE PENFRIEND

("Brevvännen")

by Britt Arenander

TRANSLATED FROM THE SWEDISH
BY MARY SANDBACH

That taste of depression in my mouth when I wake in the morning—I know it all too well. My palate nauseated, as if it had been wrestling all night with vapors from bowels that were losing the joy of life.

In the bathroom mirror I noticed a mark on my cheek, something I've made in my sleep, I thought wearily, at first. But then I fingered it, tried to smooth it out, make it disappear. I cleaned my face with cream, bathed it in ice-cold water, dried it carefully, and looked once more in the mirror. It was still there.

I had no time to smear on a face-pack to see if that would get rid of the miserable little dent. You see, an interesting new job was awaiting me. I'd had a rest for a few days, but now my cash had dried up, bills were unpaid, so yesterday I'd called the Secretarial Agency to ask if there was anything going. Yes, indeed, a Japanese export firm needed temporary help for one week, perhaps two. Their secretary was in bed with influenza. From time to time the Secretarial Agency advertises the advantages of working for them: interesting and varied duties, never any time to get tired of your place of work. Perhaps not, unless like me, you were bored from the first. But I had to do something to make ends meet. If I didn't need to pay the rent, and keep the refrigerator pretty well stocked for Martin and me, I should never do a stroke of work. But of course I can't tell anyone that. Not even Martin. I don't want to undermine my son's public spirit. That's not my job. If later on he happens to start undermining it himself I shall give him a sympathetic smile. But he's only fourteen and working hard at school. He wants to become a vet in due course, and why should I sabotage his efforts with my quite private idiosyncrasies?

In the subway I became aware that the impregnated taste in my palate had not gone, in spite of morning coffee and teeth cleaning. Probably the mark on my face had not gone either. I tried to read the morning paper, to stop myself sinking into boredom with the underground advertisements, or into despair over all the pale, tired, isolated faces about me. But I could not get the words to hang together. My chest and throat were vibrating with an indefinable feeling of anguish, and when I feel like that I have to make an effort to keep afloat. I step a bit aside from myself, as it were, and try to make fun of my temporary condition. At the same time, I promise myself that when this day is over, when I have written letters, and answered the telephone, and made coffee for the Japanese for eight hours, and when I have got home and had dinner with Martin, and when he has gone to bed, then, and only then, will I let my anguish gush out, and I shall uncork a whole bottle of wine, and smoke a whole pack of cigarettes, and weep and wail, and think up how I can most easily take my life.

The Japanese office turned out to be an admirable place of work. What a pity that influenza was the only reason for their secretary's temporary absence. Why wasn't she expecting a baby? Why hadn't her husband got a job in Singapore which had obliged her to leave? I should have taken her job as secretary without hesitation. During the whole day I wrote out three very simple letters, did a translation of a short article from a business paper, and then, between whiles, spent my time on my own reading matter, filled in an application for a sailing course for Martin, and began in a preoccupied way to put together an advertisement intended to be inserted under the heading "Personal." I did it mostly for fun. It gave me pleasure to avoid all the flags people usually fly in this connection: internal and external characteristics, longing for companionship, pleasant evenings at home, cultural interests, heart inclined to the left, right-wing outlook, Christian ideals, tired of being alone, sick of eating out, and God knows what. I'm neither tired of being alone nor tired of eating out, and my mental heart lies neither to the right nor to the left, but I am in fact longing for a man who can maintain sexual intercourse for longer than two minutes, and who has a minimum of independent thoughts in his skull. Just as I had put together five compromising lines of inquiry for this imaginary person, one of the Japanese came into my room with his imperturbably engaging smile and placed a neat draft of a letter on my desk, the third that day. I smiled back in my unreserved Western way, and thought what a pity it was that Mr. Tyoki was not half a meter taller. Maybe it is prejudice on my part, but I always find it hard if the man is shorter than I am.

On my way home I actually posted the advertisement. Why not, when all's said and done? Now I could postpone my orgy of anguish for a week or so.

The pressure on my chest had eased and I walked home. Martin doesn't usually get back before six. I bought some specially nice food, a bottle of red wine, and two fancy cakes for dessert. I love Stockholm in the rush hour. Shops full of people, a crush on the buses and the subway, restaurants beginning to fill. For a little while my city looks as if it was like any other normal metropolis you please, and not the peculiar setup it reveals itself to be at nine o'clock in the evening when the inner city lies deserted and scattered about on its different islands, which somehow seem to be in no way con-

nected. Just as the people don't seem in any way connected.
If I could move to some continental town with small shops
and pavement cafés I shouldn't hesitate. But I can't move
Martin, at least not yet. I must still spend many years in this
tundra town, where my friends are spread out over an unrea-
sonably large area, and where there are no natural meeting
places. Just think if there was a café where you could be sure
of meeting someone you knew if you passed by. Or if one
lived in a place where men turned around appreciatively and
noted that one was wearing something springlike. Oh yes, I
know that in countries where men do this the subjugation of
women is ten times worse than it is here. But still. It's just
that it's so damned difficult here to fall in with a man with
whom one could have an affair. I know that the prime reason
for my depression is that I have no lover.

Spring. This terrible spring, with its naked blue evenings
that never come to an end. It's easier in the winter. You lie as
if in your den, hibernating, preparing for the light, for life,
but now everything is here at once. You can't sleep in the
morning either. The sun raises itself far too early above the
windowsill and stations itself so that it can stare you straight
in the face. The beautiful icicles who lived their soundless,
averted, immobile lives have melted, and your winter coat
makes you sweat, the neckband itches, and great gray patches
of wet splash your stockings and the hem of your dress.
What is one to do after that time in merciful darkness, now,
when the personal columns of the newspapers are full of no-
tices of deaths while you, teeth clenched and reluctant, struggle to be born, and long to lie entangled in the love sheets of
spring and wail, delivered of joy. Joy. Does that word still
exist, I wonder? No, here among us there is only social in-
volvement, and responsibility, and the struggle to change society. By all means, I should not mind a change in society.
But it ought to be one where joy got a toe in too, quite of itself, not by order of those in high quarters.

Though I tried to regard my little advertisement S.O.S. as
a joke, an ironic grimace at my own expense, I was of course
unable to suppress a feeling of eager expectation. I'm sure
that everyone who puts in advertisements goes about in a
state of quivering and undefined anticipation, even those who
are only asking someone to give them a lift to their country
cottage. The advertisement came out the following Sunday,
and I was satisfied with the way I'd phrased it. It should give
a pretty clear signal that I was not immediately wanting to
see a new toothbrush beside my shabby old one, but that it
was a question of a so-called "free" relationship. On the other
hand, what I had not reckoned with was the number of men
who were interested in remaining unfettered. In my innocence I'd imagined that all the men in this country were really only out to find someone to watch the News with night
after night.

I was therefore quite staggered when the first A4 envelope
came from the newspaper with a batch of answers. Seventy-
eight of them. When Martin had gone to bed I sat down on
the sofa, poured out a glass of wine, and began to slit open
the envelopes. Fantastic. Like standing behind a pane of glass
through which you can see, but which those on the other side
don't know is transparent. There was something indecent
about all the exposures in this anonymous intimacy. And
what offers! A commercial traveler who would so much like
to have an easygoing sweetheart to meet when he came to the
capital; erotic maniacs with secret telephones and probably
fictitious Christian names; elderly men who wanted to see me
sitting half naked with my skirt drawn up on the dining-
room table while they rejoiced me with their tongues; bitter
shipwrecked people on the fringes of society; wealthy men
with their own islands in the archipelago and constant travels
abroad, who were most willing to pay for a relationship
which they would be furious to hear called prostitution.
Among all these letters there were a few you could call ap-

pealing. I was particularly attracted by one where the letter writer had enclosed a photograph. I sat for a long time regarding a face that was not especially beautiful but, all the same, attractive. Continued, and made the acquaintance of a man who owned his own business in Åkersberga, and who seemed to regard the whole matter as settled; a virile Portuguese who wanted to have a woman of his own to worship; a modest man with general interests who thought life would be pleasanter if you were two; and then I returned to the man with the photo. He lived in Gävle and was the staid father of a family, with a frigid wife, and now and then he had reason to visit Stockholm. In my advertisement he thought he recognized someone like himself. It did not sound too bad. I gulped down some wine and lit a cigarette. There were over thirty letters left. I sat up until three in the morning, but in view of the leisurely pace of my work at the Japanese office it did not matter. When I had read all the letters I had a strange feeling of kinship with humanity. Here I sat with my sofa full of human destinies, no two were alike, all were in different ways self-surrendering, faintly or openly despairing, just as I was myself. I had almost emptied the bottle of wine and I was seized by a passionate desire to answer all the letters personally, to spin an invisible net over the whole country, a net between fellow human beings, without registration numbers, and guaranteed to be out of reach of all forms of control. The sun would soon rise. I stretched out on the sofa and pulled a quilt over myself. I had only intended to gather strength to get up and go to bed, but I fell asleep, and woke to find Martin shaking my shoulder.

"Why are you lying here?"

Oh dear! I had been deep in a dream that I was walking along an avenue, a leafy avenue. I heard birds singing. I heard the crunch of gravel under my feet. I was walking lightly and airily, and was aware of the heavy scent of grass and sun-warmed bark. Then suddenly in my dream I thought: "But it's not summer, this must be an illusion," and before I'd finished thinking I saw that the leaves were withering before my eyes, that a cold wind was blowing them away, that the whole landscape was dying, and I halted my light airy footsteps and stood alone in that gray landscape, and within me too everything was gray and dead, as if the pulse of the universe had stopped and would never beat again.

I stretched out a fumbling hand and patted Martin's pale-blue pajama leg.

"I just fell asleep here last night. Late."

Martin looked at the wine bottle.

"You drink too much, Mum."

I tried to swallow and find my voice.

"Yes I know," I said hoarsely. "I . . . I won't drink a single glass the whole week. I promise. Not a drop."

"What's this?"

Martin had picked up one of the letters from the heap I'd pushed down on the pile rug under the coffee table.

"It's, well, it's something very private. May I have it back immediately, please."

"Of course, but what is it?"

"Don't let it worry you. Can't you let me have one little secret?"

"O.K.," he said, hurt, and slouched off into the kitchen.

I collected the letters, chucked them into my wardrobe, turned the key and put it into a drawer of my desk. Then we had breakfast, and Martin tried again to find out why I suddenly had so frightfully many letters. He smelled a rat, that was quite plain.

"You see, I've been taking part in one of those chain-letter schemes," I said suddenly, and congratulated myself on my inventiveness.

Martin looked skeptical.

"I was in one too once," he said. "But I didn't get a single letter."

"No, it doesn't always work," I said feebly.

We walked together to the bus stop where Martin had to stand and wait, and I walked on to the subway. Oddly enough, I had no headache, and now, as I began to wake up a bit, I realized that I was feeling rather well. As soon as I could I would sit down and write to the man in Gävle.

At lunchtime I went out into the sunshine and mailed the letter. Then I bought a hamburger and a carton of fruit juice and sat down on the steps of the Concert House to enjoy the bustling crowds. Stockholm was really quite endurable. Of course I was risking inflammation of the bladder, but it was worth it. The spring should have its due.

The next day, my last with the Japanese, he called. At the office. As usual, I found it difficult to decide what attitude to adopt. It's nearly always impossible for me to be myself. I have an inescapable feeling that I shall frighten everyone off if I reveal my "true self," as it's called. As if, for that matter, one only had one self. I tried to assume a slightly joking, distant tone of voice to see if he could act the fellow conspirator, if he could look on the situation with a little irony. He couldn't. He sounded naïvely attractive and very eager. As it happened, he could take a day off pretty well when he liked, and if he got into his car in the morning he could be in Stockholm about lunchtime. I said that suited me splendidly, as I was not going to work the next day, and could be free anytime. I listened in vain for a note in his voice, for a choice of words that would give me a feeling of intimacy, of unexpected and welcome kinship.

Ah, well, no good expecting the impossible. If he showed that he could come up to my physical expectations, that matter of kinship could wait.

On my way home I went into the post office to collect the money sent by the previous office where I'd worked for two weeks. While the cashier was occupied with my identity card and money order I took off my sunglasses, breathed on them quickly and bent down to polish them with the hem of my dress. Someone was watching me. From my bent position I peered up and saw that a dark-haired man was standing there smiling. He looked straight into my eyes. Taken aback, I stood up awkwardly, and slowly the man's features assumed the face of someone I knew.

"Paolo!" I said incredulously.

He smiled.

"Long time since we met."

Yes, you could call it that. Eleven years, to be exact. He'd acquired a few gray streaks in his hair, he'd not shaved that morning and his stubble stood out blue-black and virile on his tired face. I clumsily gathered up the money the cashier had pushed towards me and stepped to one side.

"How are things with you?" I asked.

"Pretty good. I'm married. And you?"

He handed over an envelope through the counter window and we walked slowly out into the street. The evening sun made my eyes smart, but I didn't want to put on my sunglasses, they would have raised a barrier between us. I was bewildered by the unreality of it. Was it possible that Paolo had been living here in Stockholm all these years, and that we'd not met? Why had he never given a sign of life? The last time we'd seen each other had been at a party at the house of people we were unaware we both knew. Paolo had been back in Italy for nearly two months, and I'd been waiting for him to come back, to seek me out. And suddenly there he was among all these people, looking at me with his crooked, ironical smile.

"How long have you been in town?" I'd asked, already a bit affected by wine, and certainly with some suppressed reproach in my voice. After all, we'd been lovers for over a year. He'd said he was only going to Italy for a few weeks, and he'd not uttered a word about wanting to end our relationship.

"For a while," he'd answered cryptically.

He'd gone with his best friend, an insufferable tall character whom I suspected began to run me down the minute my
back was turned.

"You have been. Why haven't you let me know?"

"I didn't want to."

No mistaking the message. For the rest of the evening I
drank myself drunk on purpose, and ended up in bed with
someone whose name I didn't remember when I woke up in a
totally unknown flat.

That's how the great love of my life ended. There had
never been any question of deeper emotions on his side. He
even established a steady relationship with a nurse while we
were together and told me confidingly about her sexual
difficulties. She had clearly been frigid, at least at the start,
but Paolo had made a point of rousing her erotically. He had
kept me constantly informed of his progress. Oddly enough,
I had not been jealous, and perhaps that was what annoyed
him.

"Is it Marianne you've married?" I asked out on the pavement.

"No," he answered, and began to unlock a bicycle he'd
parked against a tree, and which had a child's saddle on the
carrier.

"Have you a child?" I inquired.

"Yes," he said proudly, "a son. For that matter, how is
Martin? He must be quite big by now."

"Fourteen," I said.

"You've matured," he said with his hands on the handle-
bars. "You've become a woman at last."

Gratifying news that was.

"And what was I before?"

"I don't know, a bewildered girl, perhaps."

We stood and looked at each other in the evening sunshine
and said nothing more.

"Cheers," he said at last, and began to push the bicycle into the road.

"Cheers."

I turned sharply and began to walk towards the nearest subway station. A bewildered girl! I was twenty-six in 1968, and Martin was three. I had short hair, just as fair and just as short as Martin's, and sometimes people thought he was my little brother. We'd been deserted, left alone with each other, after my divorce. The past had returned and blotted out this spring evening of 1979 with a spring evening of 1968. The same piercing spring-evening light, the same streets, the same me, really, though now I was eleven years older, and going to have lunch the next day with an unknown man, with whom I intended to go to bed if he came anywhere near my standard. In view of my long, involuntary celibacy, my standard was pretty generous.

I went to bed early, even before Martin, who was absolutely determined to watch a late sports program, and I hoped passionately that it would be 1979 when I woke next morning, that the haunted feelings aroused by my meeting with Paolo would have subsided, and that the accidentally reopened wound would soon heal.

Of course Paolo forced his way into my dreams all night. I went to a party and Paolo didn't even recognize me; I tried to phone him and constantly dialed the wrong number; I was told by someone that he was desperately ill and lay dying; and finally, in the dawn, Paolo stood before me, a bit hunchbacked, with mournful eyes, saying that he had loved me and wanted to have a child by me, but that his feelings had evaporated when I refused.

After this last dream I awoke. The room was already light, and I couldn't fall asleep again. I lay awake for two and a half hours, tried to read but couldn't concentrate. As soon as I heard that Martin was awake I got up and made our breakfast. There were still five hours left before I was due at the restaurant. I felt weak, at sixes and sevens, as if a trap had been set for me which, for some unknown reason, I could not avoid. I've seldom felt less like meeting a man. The thing I most wanted to do was to ring up Viveka, go out to lunch with her instead, and skip the agreed meeting. Roland, that was his name, only had the telephone number of the Japanese office, and he wouldn't find me there now. But then I tried to argue reasonably with myself: Why not at least have a look at him? I'd not signed any sort of contract, or had I? If he was as attractive as the photo seemed to promise, it was worth a try, wasn't it? And the fact that I was not at the moment burning with desire was due to a slight, perfectly explicable nervousness, which would disappear as soon as we started to talk to each other. Try to be adult, cool and collected, and see the funny side of the situation.

But my nervousness increased like an avalanche, and by eleven o'clock I was in a state of acute panic. The little platform of sensible reasoning had disappeared down a chasm of horror. I chain-smoked and began to hover around the refrigerator, where a bottle of white wine had been standing unopened for several days. At last I took it out and poured myself a glass. That lovely little sensation in my stomach, and hands that already trembled less. In any case, I thought, I'm not depressed. Anything is better than that. Now I'll go to town and wander a bit until the time's up. I noticed immediately that I'd used the word "time" as if it applied to my own execution. Another glass of wine to blot out the contours of "time."

I walked into several shops haphazardly and tried on a few dresses, but they were all ill-fitting, the wrong color, or badly cut.

At a quarter to one I walked past the restaurant where we were to meet and glanced in at the window. It was full, and it suddenly occurred to me that I was risking meeting someone I knew. I walked twice around the block and then I went in, hung up my coat, and made my way, like a sleepwalker, for the ladies room. Red streaks had flared up on my neck. I tried in vain to powder over them. Why to goodness was I reacting like this? I sank onto the dressing-table stool and tried to make a brief, desperate analysis: of course, I couldn't endure the feeling of being coerced. If the man in question turned out not to be my type at all, should I in some funny way feel duty-bound to spend the whole day with him? After all, he'd driven all the way from Gävle. To hell with Gävle and private motoring, I muttered, and stepped into the restaurant, red streaks and all. I must sink or swim. At rock bottom I wanted to meet a man, that was all.

He was sitting at a corner table smiling at me. I nearly swept away a bread basket on my way through the fully oc-cupied tables.

"Cheers," I said, holding out my hand before I sat down. "Marie."

"Cheers," said the man called Roland, and held out a hand covered with eczema. I pretended not to see it and shook his peeling hand firmly.

His complexion was bad too. That hadn't shown in the photo.

"I'm sorry if I'm a bit late," I said, though I knew it was exactly one.

"No, you're not late, but I came half an hour too early. I've been sitting here enjoying myself by watching people. It's fun for us country cousins to come up to the great city now and then."

The headwaiter came up with the menu and I ordered the dish I always eat at this place plus half a bottle of white wine. Thank God there was no one I knew at the table.

"Well, well," said Roland. "So this is the woman behind the exciting advertisement. I've been enormously curious about you."

I smiled rather introspectively. I was trying to imagine

how I should have reacted to this man if I'd met him accidentally in some connection. Unfortunately, I came to the conclusion that I should have been quite indifferent. A fair-
haired man with rather coarse, irregular features, a tweed
sports jacket, a tie. That alone was enough. I tried to regard
the tie as something exotic. This friendly, usually hard-work-
ing man, with a responsible job in industry, actually looked
exotic to me. Not at all the kind I usually associated with.
Wasn't there something exciting about a family man who
ventures into a world outside his daily life?

We began to eat our prawn cocktails and I quickly emptied my first glass of wine. Conversation flowed surprisingly
easily. He did not allude in any way to the reason for our
being there, just picked out the sprigs of dill and the slice of
lemon, and this, along with the wine, gave the situation an air
of absurdity which appealed to me. He told me about his
work, about his children, about his hobby, which was writing
poetry. He'd taken the opportunity to bring along some pho-
tostat copies of his productions, and he thought I should have
a look at them between my mouthfuls of prawns. If there is
one thing I find hard, it's people who come along with their
innermost thoughts and sit waiting hopefully, while they
oblige you to read them. I read. They were frightfully bad
poems, romantic, sentimental, and moreover in rhyme.

"Well," I said, as gently and neutrally as I could, "it isn't
often one reads rhyming verse these days."

"What do you think of them?"

Alas, there was no escape. His blue eyes were pathetically
filled with expectation.

"Why, they're fine," I said, hating him for forcing me to
lie. The worst of it is that I'm good at lying convincingly.

"I've also written a number of poems," I said, for now I
thought it was my turn to say something about myself.

"I've actually had them published in a few places now and
then."

"As a matter of fact, I've thought of getting someone to illustrate these poems, and then trying to interest a publisher. Do you know of a good illustrator?"

No, I didn't.

"But what do you think of the idea of getting them printed? Which publisher should I approach first?"

"Well . . . there are a number to choose from. I've no direct experience of publishers myself."

The next thing would be that he would ask me to type a clean copy of his damned rubbish.

Here I sit bang in the middle of a trap, I thought, and poured out the rest of the wine. My panic had gone. The sun was filtering in through the window to the street, and the people outside, who had not put themselves into an idiotic situation because of sexual starvation, were enjoying the spring.

Coffee and chocolate gateau. Cigarettes. The restaurant was emptying by degrees, and the staff appeared less and less frequently after the lunchtime rush. At last we were alone at our table, and by this time I had heard so much of Roland and his life that, all in all, I could have written his biography.

"Now my dear," he said at last. "Now we know each other a bit, don't you think?"

I agreed of course, in order not to complicate matters.

"Shall we look for a quieter spot?" he said, laying his red, peeling hand over mine.

The moment of truth. I could put up with his eczema, with his self-absorption and his bad poems too. If he was now proposing that we should devote ourselves to the real object of the advertisement, it must be because he judged that there were good prospects of it being a success. This demonstration of self-confidence decided matters. I agreed, without suggesting any particular location.

"Do you live far from here?" inquired my prospective lover.

"No, but I happen to have a son who will come home from school this afternoon, so it might not be such a good idea."

"I see, so you have a son too?"

"Yes, he's fourteen."

"Goodness me!"

Now he was reckoning out how old I'd been when I had the child.

"But . . . couldn't we take a room at a hotel?" he suggested.

The thought of going to a hotel in my own city exhilarated me. On many occasions I'd walked past a little hotel in the Old Town which looked continental, elegant and mysterious. Perhaps this was the right moment to get to know the place?

As it is difficult to find a place to park in the Old Town, I suggested that I should pop up to the hotel, which was in a pedestrian precinct, and find out if they had a vacant room while Roland waited in the car. As I hurried up a cobbled street the idea of flight crossed my mind for the last time. I could leave him now. I could disappear into the city crowds and forget all about Roland Lundin. But an obstinate, dictatorial voice within me nipped this excellent idea in the bud. I don't know whether this voice was my own, and whether it was maintaining that, for my own good, I ought to give the hotel room a try. It might be that everything would function splendidly between the sheets, even if I wasn't experiencing those pleasant vibrations which are usually such a good sign. Or was the voice really that of society, of its codes, it norms, the things expected of me by others? "You've said yes. It's immoral to draw back now." Perhaps it was a mixture of both. I went up to Reception in that wonderful little hotel in a half-schizoid state and asked for a double room for me and my husband, who had just come from the country. The cool, fair-haired girl behind the desk glanced at an opened book and nodded. Yes, there was a double room at the back. It cost three hundred and fifty crowns. Was she joking? No, she looked quite serious and innocent. "Including breakfast," she added.

It was a fortune, but I could not contemplate driving around town looking for a cheaper place, and ending up in some mediocre room with gray wallpaper and a Bible on the bedside table, just to save a hundred crowns.

Roland did not ask the price. He simply picked up his briefcase, put his arm under mine, and we entered the hotel as a staid country couple.

The room was delightful. The afternoon sun seeped in discreetly; a fitted carpet in old-fashioned rose-pink with an eighteenth-century pattern subdued the remains of my anxiety, and the bed was low, wide and inviting. We smiled at each other.

"This isn't just any old hotel," said Roland and embraced me. "How much does it cost?"

"Two hundred and twenty-five," I lied, and then we kissed long and deeply. Now my body began to react.

"Dear," said Roland. "You undress and wait for me in bed. I'll just wash first."

He disappeared into the bathroom, and I slowly let my clothes fall to the ground, slipped down between the cool sheets, and lay regarding the stuccowork of the ceiling. The wine, the lovely room, and my body's expectation plaited a slowly rocking hammock for me, and I closed my eyes.

Roland drew aside the coverings carefully and gazed at me before he lay down beside me. Ah, a naked man at last. His body was well-proportioned and firm and we kissed again. His hands caressed me gently, and when they slid down between my legs I felt little spasms in my vagina. I wanted him to take me there and then, but he waited. I felt that he wasn't yet hard and he took my hand and led it to his penis. After I had fondled him for a while without any noticeable result, I removed my hand and tried to blink away some scalding hot tears that were smarting under my lids.

"Wait," he said, "fondle me a little more . . . a little . . . harder."

Harder? I had another try, but now my first, spontaneous desire had gone, and the momentary little pain had given way, leaving behind it an infinite emptiness.

"Harder," he whispered, with his tongue in my ear.

I squeezed his flabby penis frantically, but now, even if it had hardened for half a second, all the pleasure would have gone. It did not harden. He insisted that I should press and squeeze, but this strenuous massage disgusted me, and moreover, I was having to struggle against rising anger over the whole situation. For a split second I had a vision of myself pummeling his penis to a scrap of meat, and again I drew away my hand.

"I can't," I said.

"Why not?"

"I'm afraid of hurting you."

"But you don't. Be kind and go on a bit longer."

Kind? No, I wasn't a kind woman, or a serving-maid, or a woman who could put her erotic longings on a low light, in the pious and sheeplike hope that a miracle would occur. My body had already withdrawn, my feelings and thoughts too, as far as that goes. I had involuntarily begun to think of trivialities, such as what I should buy for dinner for Martin and me. Why indeed should one distinguish between body, and emotion, and intellect? The whole of me was now one blind feeling of frustration, which was struggling not to give way to rage.

"You don't ask much of a man, do you, my girl," said Roland, and I discerned a note of hatred in his voice.

"No, that's true," I said, bidding farewell to all the forced politeness of the afternoon. "I was longing for a real good fuck, however awful that may sound."

The moment I'd said it I grew afraid. Would he strangle me, or only come at me with his clenched fists?

"I tried to show you tenderness and appreciation, but you only spit at that," he said.

He turned away and took a cigarette from the packet on the bedside table. My head slowly began to split with a migraine-like headache.

"Perhaps it's not so odd that you should have to advertise for a lover," he flung at me and blew a cloud of smoke at the ceiling.

"And perhaps it's not so odd that your wife's lost interest in sex," I replied.

Touché.

"You little whore!" he hissed softly.

The calm blue eyes had grown cold, and the pupils had narrowed to a threatening slit.

"Yes, I was just waiting for that," I said. "But the stab hasn't gone home, you see. That's *your* language, not mine."

"I'd take my oath that you're one of those women's lib females too."

He pulled off the coverings and jumped angrily out of bed. Then he stubbed out his half-smoked cigarette and went into the bathroom, where he locked himself in.

I lay still for a second or two with my head thumping with migraine. He didn't come back and there wasn't a sound. Without quite knowing what I was doing, I began to dress. I went up to the bathroom door and opened my mouth to speak, but at that very moment my eye fell on my coat, which was lying on one of the two dove-gray armchairs, and, as I still could not hear a thing from behind the locked door, I snatched up my coat and the handbag that lay beneath it, quietly opened the door to the corridor, and slipped down the dimly lit stairs that were covered with a soundproof carpet.

The girl at Reception was on the phone. She did not even look up as I went past.

I quickly turned up the next side alley and disappeared among all the people going home from work. My headache was already easing and I breathed deeply.

When I'd got past a few blocks I began to walk more calmly, stopped now and then to look in a shop window, listened to a street singer and dropped a few crowns in his box.

Soon Roland would be paying the hotel bill with concealed fury, taking his highly polished car, and driving home to his frigid wife in Gävle.

I would walk home slowly, through the rush hour, and wish that the spring would soon end, that the sky would not shine so luminously blue over Stockholm's Stream, and that the screeching of the gulls was not so exultantly desolate.

LINDA

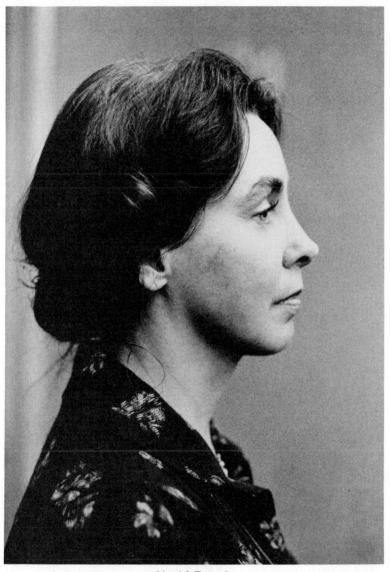

Sigrid Brunk

SIGRID BRUNK *was born in 1937 and now lives in Braunschweig, Germany. She is known for her novels* Ledig, ein Kind (Unmarried, One Child), *1972;* Das Nest (The Nest), *1975;* Der Besiegte (The Defeated One), *1977; and* Der Magier (The Magician), *1979. She has also written short stories and television plays. In 1977 she received the Wilhelmine-Lubke Prize for her novel* Das Nest.

LINDA

by Sigrid Brunk

TRANSLATED FROM THE GERMAN
BY RALPH MANHEIM

She had always had this aptitude, even as a child. Her brother had once tried to wake her by tickling, but she had just said to herself that she didn't feel a thing. The tickling had no effect, she went right on sleeping. She was aware of everything that was going on around her. She could even open her lids just a little, her eyeballs showed no sign of motion. "How spooky you look when you're asleep," a man had once said to her. "As if you were dead." He had stopped beside her bed and looked at her. She could see him perfectly. She could also see blurred shapes through her closed eyelids.

The young woman who shared her room made cooing sounds, and the baby gurgled and grunted like an animal. The door was pushed open and the nurse called in: "Looks like Fatty's asleep, he must be full!" "He's hardly taken a drop," the young woman protested. "You always bring him in when he's tired, and then he won't drink."

"He's had plenty. Come on, Fatty, you'd yell if you were hungry."

The nurse picked up the baby and left the room. In the doorway she asked in a loud voice: "Is that one still asleep?" But she wasn't asleep. She was only caught up in a dream and couldn't let it break off.

No one would understand why she had done it. A scream had been heard, they had looked for her in her room and found her in the yard down below. The bathroom window was open. They figured that she had climbed on the rim of the bathtub and forced her way through the narrow window.

It's a large yard. The leafless poplars at the back look like the fingers of a hand raised in solemn oath. And behind them? Flat country, low buildings, small factories, sheds, filling stations. This is just about the edge of the city. Then come farms and villages. It was late autumn, the sun was shining, cutting through the damp, misty air, making it visible. Spots of black mold on the earth and gravel of the yard. Through a window in the corner building one could see the African and Asian students of the midwifery school, and on the ground floor, wearing a pink kerchief, an Italian woman who worked in the kitchen. She must have been the one who let out the scream that sparked off the search.

When her husband arrived in the hospital room, they gave him her handbag, laid her coat over his arm, gathered up all the little things for him, her toothbrush, her beauty creams, her green slippers with the Lurex threads that had glittered under the Christmas tree the year before. He had wanted to give her black leather slippers, but she said she needed something warm and corny-sentimental for the long harrowing trips, the dirt and dullness of strange hotel rooms. He had also bought her a dressing gown with a swan-skin collar, she wore it in the evening after interviews, when she was trembling with excitement and fatigue. Lucie and Katie had given her a handkerchief with crocheted edging for Christmas. She had two daughters, twelve and fourteen. No one could see why she had done it.

While all these objects, which had now become utterly useless, were being stuffed into the gray carry-all that had been with her on all her trips, her husband watched the two young nurses straighten the room and unmake the bed where she had lain an hour ago, making up her mind to do it. Or had the idea come to her suddenly, when she went to the bathroom?

What had she thought of as she looked in the mirror and saw the gray, exhausted face between strands of yellow hair? What had she thought of when blood and mucus flowed out of her with her urine, when she felt her empty sunken belly, that had had a baby moving inside it only the day before? What had she thought of as she climbed on the rim of the bathtub and thrust her knees into the window niche above, where there was a roll of paper toweling, which she removed, letting it roll down into the tub? Had she looked down or looked at the sunlit windowpanes across the yard? Had she hoped the girls in the midwifery class or the little Italian woman from the kitchen would see her? Maybe she herself had screamed, though she had heard no scream. But they say a scream was heard and that's what gave the alarm. Nurses had come rushing not only to her room, but to every room in the building.

When the two young nurses took the pillows off the bed, Walter saw dark-yellowish spots in the middle of the rumpled sheet. The cloth must still be warm, he thought, the spots must still be moist. He bent over and picked up the handkerchief with the light-blue crocheted edging, which had fallen when they removed the pillows. The nurses tried hard to be still and solemn, but the most they could manage was silence. He wouldn't have minded if they had been their usual boisterous selves. What would become of the poor things if they started feeling compassion?

The day before, he had given his authorization to dissect the tiny little corpse with the big eyelids. Now he wished he had it and could lay it in her arms. That, of course, was sentimentality, but why not? She hadn't asked him what had become of the baby. She had only said, "Did you see it?" because they hadn't shown it to her. When she came out of the anesthetic, Walter was sitting beside her. She already knew it was dead, she knew it for sure. He nodded and she closed her eyes. He'd have told her later: another girl, very small, very thin, but fully formed. He thought she wanted a son, but it was all the same to her. The "little thing," "little rascal," "little goblin," "little frog"—that was what mattered to her. There it had been inside her, alive and kicking, with a will of its own, and now she had lost it through her own fault; she had killed it.

One of the nurses laid her fur coat over his arm, it smelled alive, not of fur-bearing animal but of her body, his "Linda animal." He left the room quickly.

All afternoon his phone rang. The callers wanted Walter to tell them why she had done it. He gave all sorts of answers, most of them confirming the callers' conjectures. That was the easiest way and spared him long-drawn-out arguments. Yes, yes, Linda had been run down, overworked, her nerves had been shot. Then, too, some medicine may have disagreed with her. Even in childhood she had been subject to choking fits. Maybe she had only wanted to lean out of the window for air. No, nothing organic, her heart was perfectly all right, more likely some neurosis. Anxiety. Yes, anxiety. Fear. We're all of us afraid of something.

All day the telephone rang. Relatives. Colleagues. They listed her professional accomplishments, reeled off the details of her career, as though he had hidden her and their magic words would help him to conjure her up again. They confessed their envy, confessed they had spoken disparagingly of her charm, which had admitted her to the presence of the nastiest, most inaccessible people. Walter contended that she had actually been shy. They laughed at him. Linda shy! He had to be kidding! How, if she was shy, could she have succeeded in interviewing Fidel Castro in the midst of the missile crisis? And what mean questions our dear little Linda had asked him! No, she had no reason to do this thing. She had two children who needed her love, she could have survived without a third. It could only have been nerves, a nervous breakdown.

I don't know, she cried a good deal, they should have given her something to soothe her, she cried a good deal . . .

Finally, instead of putting the receiver back in its cradle, Walter set it on the table beside the phone. Now they couldn't get at him. He ran his hand over his face and looked around. His daughters were standing in the kitchen doorway. Lucie the elder had made coffee. Both were embarrassed and intimidated. They cried and held each other's cold hands, their voices were raw and pinched, but now and then they couldn't help laughing aloud, and then they looked at each other in pale horror.

They helped him take the things out of the gray carry-all. When he opened the wardrobe doors wide and saw the dresses lined up on the rod, he thought there was one blouse he had never seen. He took it out and smelled it. It wasn't new, it had been worn. But when? Where? In some strange city or other, at dinners, at an interview with some stranger or other. Why hadn't he said: "You're going to stay home! You can't travel in your condition." But she wouldn't have listened. She would have said: "Other women have to work. They have to stand behind the counter all day in the exact same condition."

He clutched the strange, familiar-smelling blouse, shut the door, and pressing the blouse to his face flung himself on the bed. There were spots on the wall beside the bed, a squashed fly, finger marks. That was their signal. He slept in the adjoining room, and when she was afraid or felt sick at night, or when she wanted to speak to him, she beat her fist against the intervening wall. On books, cupboard doors, on the mirror, he would long find the marks of her lotion-moist hands.

She had taken hold of some things so often that they were dark from the oil they had absorbed.

He lay on her bed, pressed the blouse to his eyes, and stopped thinking. He was exhausted. Now he was neither sad nor desperate, only tired, dead tired. Why had she done this to him? Why had she done it?

When she woke up at night, she was usually lying on her right side. The window was open, and she felt a cold draft on her neck. On the wallpaper in front of her she saw blurred spots, the light of the street lamp dispersed by the blackening leaves of the pear trees and reflected by the mirror. When she turned on to her back, the whole room was broken up into spots of light, a heavy snowfall, great flakes of light all around her, shivering and shaking with every stirring of the leaves. A soft crackling and scratching when one dead leaf grazed another. A persistent rustling accompanied the shadows that moved across the wall in vanishing stripes. Soft sounds of paper and leather. The smell of the smoke, oil and soot with which the fog blankets us.

She awoke every night at two. Then she waited for the baby's movements, laughed at the thought of them, and tried by running her hand over her groin to see if it was a foot, knee or head that swelled out the skin for a moment before diving under. She rolled over on the left side, so as to have the whole room in her field of vision, and to feel the wintry air on her forehead. She felt her heartbeat in her ears and temples. The water glass on the bedside table showed two dividing lines that shimmered white; the luminous hands on the clock were paler. A train raced through the night. The trains that circled the city in a wide arc had always given her a sense of peace. Feeling safe and snug in her bed, she fell asleep again.

A farm boy found three newborn kittens in among some old horse blankets, still bloody and wet and plastered with the mother cat's hair. Hissing, the mother fled into a corner cluttered with a harrow and horse's harness. Unable to contain his joy, the boy runs across the yard and reports his enormous discovery to a man. The man looks up for a moment, more through the boy than past him, and takes a few more shovelsful of sand. Then, carrying the shovel horizontally, he follows the boy, who is hopping with eagerness. The kittens are lying there like dark wet worms, bloody and blind. Will the man be pleased? Will he laugh? Will he bend down to get a better look at them? The boy shifts from foot to foot and rubs his knees. He has never seen such tiny kittens. The sun is high in the sky.

The man is right there. Only for a second has the boy been in front of him, looking at the kittens on the old leather-bordered blankets, he has only this one second for his joy and friendship with the man. The shovel is lying loose in the man's hands. Once he gets there, he shoves it playfully under the wet, naked bodies. He gives the handle a jerk and they tumble onto the blade; one rolls over on its back, it's a male, he has a naked pink belly and a tiny penis.

The man moves the shovel back into a horizontal position and without looking at the boy goes back across the yard. The sun is high in the sky. The boy looks at the kittens and then up at the man's face. He stumbles and laughs, his laughter is loud and unnatural, he wants to infect the man with it, he wants a response from the man, a laugh or a wink of connivance. Aren't they cute? Aren't they tiny?

But the man doesn't laugh. He doesn't even seem to see the boy. He doesn't hurry especially but heads with an air of purpose for the narrow ditch with the ducks swimming in it. Even before reaching it, he slowly advances the shovel, raises the handle slightly and lowers the blade. Still slippery with their mother's mucus, the kittens slide off, the water hardly splashes, they sink instantly. They don't stir, only their ears and their skinny tails quiver in the current. Long after they should have been dead, one of them twitches with its hindquarters, its paws keep twitching and twitching.

That woke her up. It was the child inside her, the stranger, kicking or punching. But the image of the drowned kittens wouldn't go away. She saw the little boy standing beside the ditch. The tears were running down his cheeks, but it didn't occur to him to reach into the water, gather up the bundle of dark-gray bodies, and lay them in the grass. Behind his back he heard the screams of the mother cat, she circled around him in a wide arc and her yellow eyes didn't let go of him. She thinks I'm the murderer, he thought. But I'm not the murderer.

Her husband was sleeping in the next room. Sometimes when it was very still, when the window was closed and her senses were sharpened by listening, she could hear his breathing through the wall. She could hear her children too. Not wanting to wake from the sleep that protected her from such thoughts and fears, she crossed the hallway on her bare feet and listened to their breathing.

Now Walter is sleeping in the next room again; her bed still bears the imprint of his body, her blouse is lying crumpled on the floor. He is sleeping in the sour smell that his bedclothes take on when he is tired and sweaty. Around the index finger of his left hand he had twined a lock of her hair that he has found on the carpet. He has wound it taut and scraped it with his right thumbnail until it's as smooth and cool and hard and shiny as living hair.

In the middle of an interview about the missile crisis—in which tempers threaten to get out of control at any moment —Fidel Castro had asked whether her blond hair was real. The question was intended to throw her off balance, and it did. Her reaction was too harsh and priggish: "In my country one doesn't ask a woman such questions." She felt the wind blowing through her hair, pushing up yellow, too yellow strands of it against the blue of the sky. The dictator had thrust his hands under his broad cartridge belt, the collar of his jacket was turned up, his cap pushed back, his curly black beard, in the midst of which his lips looked unpleasantly red, wobbled as from his exalted position he hurled insults at her and Europe and America. She interrupted the torrent of slogans: "It's true: my hair is bleached. They say you won't dare ask for Russia to help."

"There are Russian warships armed with nuclear missiles right off our coast," he said with a smile.

"I hear they've changed course, I hear they're going away."

"Who says that!" he shouts in uncontrollable rage. "Who said that? That's American propaganda!"

An interviewer must provoke. But he must be careful not to arouse hatred. He must never drive the interviewee into such a tight place that his only thought is to strike back. Such duels are useless. They shed no light and reveal no truth. And yet, how exciting it is to get a man so upset that he reveals more of himself than he wants to or realizes.

It was just this latent antagonism between the sexes that made her interviews so popular. But it involved her in great risks. Since she taped her interviews, her defeats as well as her victories came to the ears of the public. Of course she could have cheated, she could have erased and spliced, but to that she would not stoop. She took pride in giving blow for blow, in parrying quickly enough to turn defeat into victory. Since defeat means defeat as a woman, since she was fighting for her sex, it was the man in her antagonist that she had to overcome. Her best interviews were those that left both parties exhausted and reconciled; a tie was her greatest triumph. She had to go into battle as supple as a fencer. She fell in love with nearly all the men she fought. She recognized the erotic character of her willingness to endure blows, to let herself be wounded; she had no illusions. Of course she wouldn't have admitted it, except to the man in question, but he knew without being told. She had to lay herself open, to sit passive and still, all eyes for his least movement, all ears for the slightest change of inflection, and like a woman in love she had to know exactly how she could wound him. And she had to bear in mind this rule: The more powerful the man she was tormenting with her questions, the more imposing not only his position in life but his physical build as well, the more quickly and brutally he would strike back. This may sound like a simplification, but she had never met a large, powerfully built man who did not sooner or later try to trample her. Such men probably held that a weak woman had no right to a fighting spirit. They sensed her proneness to nervous collapse. Her combination of fragility and wit infuriated them. Some were ashamed when they realized how they had let themselves go. But their shame soon turned to arrogance. The only man in whom she aroused no hate was Walter.

He lay on his side, convulsed, digging his teeth into sleep and forgetfulness, his legs drawn up and his arms folded over his chest like an embryo. Then he turned over on his back, stretched his legs, sighed. His pajamas lay on the carpet, he was sleeping in his underwear. He had also tossed his suit carelessly on the floor. But on the chair by the window lay a fresh shirt, and over it a black tie. He had laid out black socks as well, and he would wear not the red enamel cufflinks, but the silver ones inherited from his grandfather. He locked his hands under his head and looked up at the ceiling, which was gray and streaked with dust. They had planned to have it done over in the spring. His room was ugly, the furniture had been chosen at random, the colors didn't harmonize. She should have made him a better home, she hadn't taken good care of him; he was thin, his hair was gray.

When they married, they had remodeled an old farmhouse at the edge of town. They could have torn it down, but they were romantic. It consists of only four large rooms and a small outbuilding, where Walter has his studio. The house is painted white and surrounded by an apple orchard. All around it modern houses have gone up, even two high-rise buildings, but all they needed was a place to hang their hats, they had no time for so-called gracious living.

Though she had been a burden to Walter, he now feels forsaken, like an abandoned child. He's afraid of his daughters, who look at him out of their dark eyes, questioning and pleading for help. What is he to say to them? And what is he to say to all the people who ask questions on the phone? And what is he to say to himself in answer to the perpetual question: Why?

He has already attempted so many answers. None is right. Their marriage was not unhappy. Those who thought so, and a lot of people did, were mistaken. She was not at a difficult age for women; or if she was, she didn't know it. The embittered man who claimed there was no such thing as a happy woman of forty would only have made her shrug. She had no time to notice that she was forty.

For the present Walter could think of only one answer: I shouldn't have let her travel alone. All alone in a dreary hotel room, she sat on the edge of the bed, clasping her belly in her arms to hold the child fast. There was no longer the elegant, ironic Linda; she had become an animal, a frightened female gorilla, cradling her unborn child in her belly, clasping it in her arms, unwilling to let it go. The radiators clanked, somebody's bath water from upstairs gushed down through the drainpipe, toilets flushed by strangers gurgled and roared. When she switched on the light in the bathroom, cockroaches fled into dark corners, and later, when after lying awhile in the dark she switched on the bedside lamp, one of the black creatures, engaged in climbing the wall beside her bed, lost its hold and fell. She screamed and started searching the bed sheets.

She had given Walter a detailed description of this hotel room in London. He visualized it when she told him that on her last trip she had arrived late, too tired to look for acceptable quarters, and had had to content herself with a sleazy room in a cheap hotel. Actually, it was the kind of hotel room he liked best. But he always saw her sitting timidly on the edge of the bed, saw cockroaches crawling over tiles, heard the tempestuous flushing of toilets, saw milky white condoms in the corners of the room or half hidden by ivy on the window ledge outside. All third-class hotels have the same drawbacks.

But never before had she lived through such a night as that one in Frankfurt, the day before the death of her child. It was the night of November 22, she was sitting on the edge of the bed, clasping the child tight. One may wonder why she didn't get dressed, pay her bill and go home, why she waited until the next day, and then drove four hundred kilometers, as though glued to her seat, pressing her buttocks and thighs into the cushions, as if that could seal up her body, which was racked with terrifying shooting pains. She tried in vain to remember the labor pains she had had before Lucie and Katie were born. What did this new pain mean? Was she going to lose her child now in the sixth month, or was it something harmless that would pass? That was why she had waited through the night, to lull the pain and quiet her nerves. But without success. In the presence of the man she had come to interview, she was seized with sobs and couldn't stop them. They tore at her insides. She was bleeding, her life blood was seeping away. No man had ever struck her so telling a blow, she would never recover. When she had said to Walter, "Other women have to work in the exact same condition," he had no way of knowing that she was lying to him, just as she was trying to deceive herself. She had been spinning herself into a cocoon of lies, pretenses, and sensible-sounding arguments, such as: "Once the baby is here, I won't have time to interview this man. He has just reached the interesting point in his career, when everyone is asking: Will he make it or will he fail? Could it be that he's washed up? In a few weeks everyone will know. But they want to know *now*."

That had sounded convincing. Those were facts that no one could deny. And she had lulled herself with them, repeated them over and over again. It was none of anybody's business that this man, whom she had interviewed exactly two years before, had bewitched her, that she simply had to see him again. As a reporter, she always stuck to facts, she had made a fetish of them, nothing mattered but what could be verified and proved. If she said something in public she had to be able to substantiate it. This was her professional creed, she had never thought it burdensome; on the contrary, it had become the law of her life, a sort of philosophy. But below the surface she dreamed more and more; daydreams, erotic fantasies, excursions into the irrational had begun to take up more and more of her time. She became less active, slept longer than before, or lay in bed awake, talking to herself. Her gait had changed, the children's questions annoyed her, their schoolwork, which up until then she had followed with the interest of a sports fan, began to bore her, her affection for them came to seem mechanical. She had often quoted Cocteau's words, "A glass of water enlightens the world," and spoken of "sacred reason." Now she saw the glass of water as a shimmering crystal ball which refracted the light and cast mysterious reflections.

She realized that the desire to see this man whom she had once interviewed was a part of her subliminal life, but she saw no danger in this other life; she looked on it rather as an easing of discipline, a kind of holiday trip for the mind. She justified her erotic fantasies by telling herself that reality was stronger, that she wasn't undercutting reality, but only taking a bit of a rest from it. Nor was she taking anything from Walter—wasn't she carrying his child? She had never been physically unfaithful to him. What difference did her secret dream life make? Could anyone ever know? Wasn't she innocent?

At their last meeting she had seen that the man liked her and would have liked to "have" her.

In these two years of unbroken erotic tension she had become pregnant again, though she had given up expecting it. Sometimes it seemed to her that the child in her womb was by the other man. And just as she had sometimes taken her daughters with her on the pretext of showing them an interesting city, a foreign country, but in reality in order to highlight her womanhood, she was now impelled to show her rounded body to make him aware of the fullness of her life, to impress him, to win his respect. He, however, was only irritated by the sight of her rounded form, modeled by the folds of her ample dress.

She had started by asking him two or three questions, feeling him out, looking for the right tone. While getting her bearings in the large, high-ceilinged room with the black leather furniture and bare uncurtained windows, she had laughed, leaned back in her chair, stirred her coffee, and barely glanced at the man. They had exchanged a few words of small talk. Later she would keep her eyes open for his hidden reactions. For the present she was only trying to get the feel of him. But already he struck.

At that moment all the questions she had meant to ask him struck her as pointless. Automatically she switched on the tape recorder; to regain her composure she picked up her handbag, took out the file cards on which she had jotted his outstanding achievements and drafted a few questions. These she prepared to read off, something she never did, a technique she had always scorned and ridiculed in others, since sticking to a program kills intuition. Suddenly she realized that her trip had been a mistake. She turned the file card this way and that and in a hoarse voice asked a pointless question that he didn't answer. The tape was running, but all it recorded was breathing. When Walter listened to the tape later on, it told him nothing.

After a long silence the man's voice said: "Well well!" The next sound was her sobs.

There is concern, but also disdain in the man's voice: "How could you travel in this condition? What's the good of it? Are you *mad?* Can't you see that you're too far gone? You'll only crack up. And accomplish nothing. Nothing whatever!"

She knew that he only said all this to disconcert her. Never had she been treated so unfairly. Taking advantage of her pregnancy to demolish her as an interviewer!

"You come here and demand answers! You claim them as a right! What have you to offer in return?"

"Asking questions is my job."

"That's no excuse," he said.

A pause. Then again the man's voice:

"If something I've said has made you cry, I want to apologize."

"There's no need to."

"But tell me. What has upset you so?"

"You."

"Thank you."

Then silence. Her stifled voice says: "I want to go now. I can't talk anymore."

To Walter the whole conversation was a mystery. He slipped the tape into its cassette, put it in a desk drawer and resolved to forget it.

That night in the hotel room she had run it several times. Through the partly open window poured the noise of a city street with an active night life—bars, nightclubs, a movie house. Every ten minutes a streetcar came screeching around the bend, its bell clanging as it approached the stop that was right under the window, and clanging some more as it started up again. No sooner was it gone than new groups formed— men singing and bellowing while waiting for the next car, and shouting at every girl who passed. People seemed to be shouting from one end of the street to the other, the voices broke against the walls, swelled in the narrow canyon, and rose up to her many times refracted and for that reason unintelligible. In the morning she saw there were apartments high above the shops and offices, and saw women in dressing gowns watering flowers and shaking out bedclothes. Had they got used to the noise, or was it really quiet enough up there to make sleep possible?

Her room was on the second floor. Panic-stricken, she had thrown her coat around her and was listening to the man's soothing and infinitely contemptuous voice on the tape: "Are you *mad?* Can't you see that you're too far gone? You'll only crack up and accomplish nothing!"

Had she been mad to risk the life of her child by taking this trip? Could it be that her ambition verged on madness? Wasn't there something obsessive about this profession that filled her life and left her hardly any time for her husband and children, about the career she worked at without consideration for her health? Hadn't she neglected to live? She had been neither a good mother nor a good wife, she had had no time for either one. Her children and her husband had often got on her nerves, and she hadn't had self-control enough to hide it. How often she had said: "Kindly leave the room and shut the door behind you." When she wanted to work undisturbed she had hung a red cardboard disc on her doorknob—her red light. She planned new interviews and wrote up old ones; she went looking for interesting personalities, wrote for newspapers, spoke for broadcasting stations. In that Frankfurt hotel room she realized how absurd her life had been, how she had wasted herself on an unworthy aim. She clasped the child in her arms, cradled it, and said over and over again: "Leave me the child at least, don't take everything away from me, leave me the child."

In Treblinka they cut a pregnant woman's belly open. The fetus fell from the wound. She bent down as though to gather water in both hands, picked up the child, put it back into the gaping wound, and collapsed.

"Don't think about it anymore, forget it," said Walter when she awoke from the anesthetic. There were deep shadows under his eyes. His child was dead. She had killed his child.

"Don't think about it, forget it, go back to sleep!" But he doesn't hear her, never again will he hear her. And never again would he want to hear her, to feel her presence. She knows the kind of woman she was. Only yesterday she would have said: "The visible world is enough for me." She would have shut out the dead and any claim they might raise. We cry because something has been taken away from us. We don't want it back again in a different, unfamiliar form. We want it back the way it was, or not at all. We are afraid of having it change.

Walter pushed the bedspread aside and swung out his legs. He supported himself on his left elbow, and the effort of swinging his body around made him raise his head. The sinews on his neck stood out. How thin his neck was! When he set his feet on the floor and pushed his shoulders forward, his head drooped onto his chest. He yawned, cleared his throat, rubbed his eyes. Then, blinking, he looked toward the window, saw the white shirt, the black tie; his gaze became rigid, empty.

"Go on sleeping. You don't have to think about it yet. Lucie and Katie are still asleep or pretending to be, they're just as much afraid of the day as you are. They're just as much afraid of seeing you as you are of seeing them. They're afraid you'll cry. It frightens daughters to see their father cry, they'd like to mother him, to comfort him like a small child, but they have a horror of acting like women, they don't want to be women yet, not for a long time. A word, a chord, a beam of light can make them soft or hard, they don't know yet what it's right to show, to admit, and what must be hidden. So go on sleeping, escape into sleep."

But then he got up for good and changed his underwear.

His body is trim, delicately formed, he seems younger than he is. His face is narrow, the blue eyes behind rimless glasses have a childlike look, but their naïveté is put on. He is much more complicated than one would think. Yes, indeed, complicated, aloof, secretive. He keeps everything at a distance, he has no desire for power and has no power to defend. In the morning he goes into his studio or drives to the Academy. He fills his pipe and slips into the leather jacket that he never buttons. But today he dresses up, puts on his black suit.

While tying his tie, he discovered the lock of hair he had twined around his finger. He pushed it off, examined his finger, rubbed it for a moment, and laid the ring of yellow hair on the smoking table beside his notes for the Amenophis film he was planning to do as soon as the Mozart film was finished. He had returned from Egypt only three months before.

In the hallway he saw the receiver still lying beside the phone and, horrified at his absentmindedness, put it back in its cradle. Then he hesitated for a moment as though expecting a phone call, a voice that would say: "For God's sake, Walter, what's wrong? I've been trying to get you for five hours, I was going to call the police." But the phone was silent. Later, he straightened the room. He took the blouse, smoothed it out and put it back on the hanger. At ten the cleaning woman rang. He sent her away.

"Has Mom had an automobile accident?" asked Lucie, who was helping him.

"What gave you that idea?" But then he remembered: the girls had heard their mother drive up, they had heard her call him to come out and get her because she couldn't move from the seat where she'd been sitting for five hours as though glued. But they had no way of knowing what had happened in Frankfurt, so they had thought of some accident on the *Autobahn*.

"No," he said. "It wasn't an automobile accident. You knew you were getting a little sister, didn't you . . ." What a way to talk to his big daughters! Exasperated, he cut himself short.

"That's what Mom died of," he said finally.

Later on, Lucie and Katie talked it over. "Mom died of the baby. Did you know that?"

"Yes, but where's the baby?"

"When the mother dies, the baby dies too," said Lucie precociously.

They sat whispering in their room under a picture of Pierre Brice and came to the conclusion that a woman of forty was too old to have a child.

"She really *was* forty!"

"And Walter was fifty!" Katie whispered.

"That doesn't matter, silly."

That led to an argument. Katie insisted that it did matter, an old father's "material" wasn't so good. They stopped talking when they heard the phone. Walter answered and again they heard him saying: "No, I don't know either. I wish I did. I blame myself. She was run down, overworked. And maybe having this child wasn't such a good idea. But who thinks of such things?"

All day long there were visitors. On the pretext that the house was in disorder, he took them into his room and moved the papers, folders and ashtrays back and forth, without any noticeable improvement.

A man was sitting in the armchair under the standing lamp, a colleague from the newspaper where she had started out. He was tormenting Walter with the mindless simplifications that might have explained "everything" to a total stranger but could only baffle anyone who knew her. He quoted her as saying: "Show plenty of self-assurance, don't let them put you off—then you'll get everything you want." What non-

sense! What had she got? Naturally, in her profession you
had to make a show of self-assurance. Then at least you have
a chance. But it's no guarantee of success.

And again he quoted her: "Success suddenly changes a
person's whole life. But only for a day. You're a sprinter
doing the hundred-meter dash. You cross the line, you win.
And then what? You have to start all over." When he heard
that, the man said, he knew it would end in tragedy.

Walter had listened, nodding, to these explanations. "She
was very ambitious," the man said hesitantly. "She was ice
cold, as hard as nails. When we men gave up, Linda barged
in. She could interview anyone she pleased. It amused her to
get interviews out of men who were known to hate the press,
who had sent others away. When others said, 'He's a hopeless
case,' Linda's curiosity was aroused. She kept at it till she got
what she wanted."

Walter, who had just nodded, stood holding the bottle, on
the point of pouring the journalist a fifth or sixth drink.
With a look of skeptical astonishment, he studied the profile
of his visitor, the lips sucking at a cigarette stub, the over-
heated dark-red cheeks, the blue eyes staring at the carefully
cultivated length of white ash. He wasn't aware of Walter's
glance, didn't see Walter put the bottle down, put one hand
in his trouser pocket, and stand waiting in the middle of the
room.

"It's a hard job," said the visitor. "A man's job. But that
didn't frighten Linda."

Walter didn't trouble to tell his visitor about the nights
when they had sat on the bed together in the cold room,
when he had slowly and patiently cleared away her fears and
complexes, as though removing rubble from good, fertile soil.
Time and again, a new layer of rubble formed, it seemed to
fall from the sky. And good God, the things she had said:
"I'm probably a nymphomaniac. Instead of rolling on the
floor with men, I wrestle them with words and ideas. I'm

probably a sadist, or maybe a masochist. I goad them to make them beat me. My ambition comes from an inferiority complex, that's why I always pick the beastliest, most brutal men, who would throw anyone else out, not me though, or not right away, but only when they've worked off their aggressions on me."

Wrapped in a blanket, he sat on the edge of her bed. Sometimes when anger overcame him, the jagged vein on his temple swelled, but nothing he said showed that he was angry. Even as a child she had wished she could read thoughts. It had always interested her more to know what people *think* than what they do. And when she fathomed someone's thoughts, she felt that she was taking part in Creation. Her greatest pleasure was watching people and noticing gestures they themselves were hardly aware of. It was not only her greatest pleasure, it was an addiction. No better than drug addiction, no better than chasing after dreams.

"Don't reproach yourself," said Walter. "Everything is all right."

But her last fears, the terrors of her last hours—these she wouldn't be able to discuss with him.

It's a large yard. The leafless poplars at the back are like big upright fingers. And behind them? Flat country, low buildings, small factories, sheds, filling stations. The little Italian woman with the pink kerchief could be seen putting some metal object, that flashed in the sunlight, on the kitchen window ledge to dry. Two floors higher, in the corner building, the midwifery class. The crowns of the students' heads were smooth and dark, madonna-like; they had red dots in the middle of their foreheads, or else they had frizzy blue-black hair and skins the color of café-au-lait, and their cows' eyes looked grave and wise. In the left wing, three floors higher, a woman in a thin white nightgown that blew in the wind like a light summer dress, crouched in the narrow bathroom window. She filled the whole window space. Like a picture in a frame. Her hair was strikingly yellow, it glittered in the slanting rays of the sun. It had been bleached a little too garishly. She leaned forward as though to gather water from a pool far below her. As if a blond woman in a summer dress had wanted to gather water in both hands. No one could see why she had done it.

YOUTH

("Gioventù")

Flaminia Morandi

FLAMINIA MORANDI *was born in Rome on March 11, 1947. She took her degree in literature at the University of Rome, with a thesis on Italian literary journalism in the early years of the twentieth century.*

After a period of work in the movies as a script girl, she was in the press office of the Italian Radio, interviewing important figures in radio and television. She made her own radio debut as co-author, with Maurizio Costanzo and Dina Luce, of a popular series of broadcasts in the 'sixties, "Buon Pomeriggio." She has been associated with radio ever since, and has made an occasional venture into television. Among other productions, she was responsible for "Sala F," a feminist broadcast devoted to women's problems, and for "Radio 3131," a very popular general program lasting three and a half hours at a time, with listeners calling in. For radio she wrote also eight monologues for women, which were performed by eight famous Italian actresses.

She is married to the journalist Maurizio Costanzo and has two children.

YOUTH

("Gioventù")

by Flaminia Morandi

TRANSLATED FROM THE ITALIAN
BY WILLIAM WEAVER

I could begin anywhere. This story is entirely personal and will never serve as an example, a model, to anyone. Perhaps what I remember best is the end, an end that for the two of us—but I should say the three of us, as in a proper domestic triangle—was the real beginning.

We arrived in Benares from Delhi at dawn, on the Taj Mahal Express. The heat was in abeyance. The sky was pink, without a sign of monsoon. Virginia had been slightly hurt in our first accident on Indian soil. A scooter-taxi, taking us to the bazaar, turned over in the midst of the crowd. Bleeding, the driver pursued us all the way to the hospital, to demand his five rupees fare, and not even the policeman was able to get rid of him. The accident made us miss the plane for Benares.

In our "conditioned chair" car, nobody managed to sleep, or even talk. Virginia's arm was in a scarf-sling. I changed my skirt for a pair of Indian cotton slacks which hid the bruises on my thigh.

We had learned the news practically by chance, reading a newspaper.

Luca was dead: it was not clear whether by accident or by suicide. The body had been found on a little deserted island, a few kilometers outside Benares. The news was already some days old, because he had left his identification behind in his room at the Hotel de Paris, and the proprietors had waited awhile before deciding to inform the police.

A few days later, since there were no next of kin, the Embassy released the information and told the papers.

We set off at once, a disastrous flight: twenty-two hours, with endless stopovers in Tehran and Kabul. Formalities, missed connections. Finally we reached Delhi, at dawn, of course, and between dawns we had not slept one minute.

Both Virginia and I (but who am I? I don't want to have a name in this story: I will simply be the person telling it) had a letter with his last wishes and bequests, written in his own hand some years before. Our possession of such a private letter, in two copies, almost identical, or rather absolutely identical in form, plunged Virginia into one of her silences that could go on for days or months. But she and I came to an agreement, in any case: we would leave together. At this point everything was ending (or beginning, as I said before). Though we had known each other since childhood, for thirty years more or less, this was our first trip together. There was some awkwardness in acting as a pair, coordinating every action, and still, though the occasion was anything but happy and Virginia's silence was quite unshakable, a strange excitement made us hasten, dash to Fiumicino, buy newspapers, find our seats (after an exhausting delay) on the Pan Am plane.

It was at Fiumicino, as I was buying the papers, that I observed Virginia carefully. She was almost the same as in the past: tall, thin, her hair in waves that never became curls. Her eyes big, the lashes accentuating the steady absence of her gaze. And in that absence, a painful, fragile impression, as if she were on the verge of tears, even when she was smiling. A single gesture had remained precise from childhood: her tireless twisting of her hair between the forefinger and middle finger of her right hand. An almost bizarre elegance in her clothes, chosen at random, but all alike in an infallible taste for subtle colors that made you forget even the cut of the dress. She wore colors like signals of her humor or mood. With me everything was louder, more deliberate, more expectable, predictable. My colors were bright, created specially so people would notice them, and this was surely a reaction to my basic shyness. Only Luca, from the start, had realized how this display hid a fundamental insecurity that changed, then, into aggressiveness and obstinacy.

All during the flight Virginia kept eating the pistachios bought in Tehran, washing them down with mineral water. I ate the badly cooked dishes of the various Eastern countries we were flying over, or where we made a stop. I had never been to the Orient, but Virginia had made two trips to India with Luca, when our stories had already become entangled.

To see now those places that in my imagination had once made me suffer, filled me with a strange anxiety, a desire to spill everything I had kept repressed for fifteen years. But it was impossible to find any way of communicating with Virginia; it was as if she were sleeping; and I ceaselessly asked myself if she was thinking about those trips of hers with Luca, when the two of them had reached such a fine understanding that he could maintain a perfect equilibrium between the two of us. An emotional equilibrium, I mean, because I don't believe that, by then, they still went to bed together, even though I can't be sure, and Luca's words always had the effect of making more obscure things that were already clear and established.

Luca's body, lifeless, or rather motionless, in the evening light of the little island in the Ganges, appeared to me like a sequence in an Oshima film, *The Ceremony*. A stupendous and frightening sequence. Fom the boat you glimpse an uninhabited hut, and inside, as you gradually approach, in a long shot, the body of a dead man, an absurd color, red as a lobster; a swelling, a violence that clashes with the blue of the deep water, with the dark green covering the mountains all around. I don't remember exactly if it was the sea or a river; only the sensation of walls looming over the little island. Walls that cut off the light and made it vibrate like certain mountain streams, when evening falls and nothing remains in the sky but a luminescence that is the lingering memory of the day now gone and gone forever.

Luca was also gone and forever, as he wanted, leaving to the two of us, with identical letters, the final commission of his going: "I want my body to be burned, wherever it may be. And, in the urn, there must be placed some bay leaves from the Palatine, not because of poetic glory but as an homage to the city that has given me most. Then the urn must be emptied into the waters of the Ganges, before the Kali Gat of Benares."

Yes, Luca was very romantic and this business of the bay leaves was apparently a demand for recognition of the effort his works had cost him. Works that not many had read, though there were naturally the "happy few," determined to consider him the finest writer of his time. Virginia and I were also among them, but the bay leaves made me smile, suggesting the kitchen, and I'm convinced that Virginia, while she read my letter that was exactly like hers, was thinking the same thing.

In Benares it was too early to find a café open, so we decided to wait a little while in the station. Some soldiers were vigorously cleaning their teeth with a little wooden stick, like liquorice, spitting on the tracks. A hygienic practice effective against cavities, according to the infallible Hindu prescriptions. I had read about it, but to see them actually doing it gave me the first genuine impression of having set foot in India, a continent that for me, until that moment, had been only the scene of the loves of Luca and Virginia, when I had remained on a beach crammed with tourists, as I waited for a letter that never came.

Outside the station buffet we were accosted by a fake holy

man, a sadhu with hennaed hair, complete with breech-clout and a three-pronged pitchfork for driving away demons. He was French, lost for six years on the hills around Benares, his passport and visa long since expired. Without a cent, he was now anxious to get back to Bombay to look for his wife. We bought two silver bracelets from him for a hundred rupees and an apple. "Never refuse to give alms," Luca used to say. "Begging is a job like any other, and it should be paid, as we pay for any professional performance that interests or amuses us. Arousing compassion in others is a science. True, we've made great progress in the art of pain, from Stendhal on, but India has achieved eternal perfection."

Luca always enjoyed quoting Stendhal. He enjoyed saying that the French writer was the last impassioned spirit, and Luca wanted to be born a second time only to meet Clelia Conti, among the lemon or orange trees of the Chartreuse, I can't remember which.

In Benares everything seemed to me already familiar, not because I recognized a street or a monument, lost among the golden rooftops or the muddied beggars, holding a leaf in their hand, and not from the stories of Luca or Virginia, but because I still sensed—how to put it?—Luca's smell in those streets, in the midst of the monkeys' temple, of which he had sent me a postcard with a drawing and without a signature. The drawing was of himself carrying me in his arms, both of us naked. His expression was grim, with a sly smile that boded no good. One detail: he had drawn my face, my long black hair, but the body was Virginia's, her tiny breasts, slender thighs, delicate ankles . . . all it did was infuriate me, as usual.

Virginia now proceeded briskly, not talking. It was as if she were going to an appointment with Luca, not with a handful of ashes we had simply to throw into the river. We took a room at the Hotel de Paris. Outside, in an immense park with huge trees and huge flowers all dripping after the night's monsoon, a group of snake charmers was performing for some American tourists. Cobras, vipers swayed to the sound of the flute they didn't hear. Then it was the mongoose's turn: for twenty rupees, he split the head of a snake in the brief space of a minute.

At the hotel they seemed to have no recollection of Luca. They sent us to police headquarters, an old colonial building, in a two-seated rickshaw. And there: Luca's first mystery. It couldn't have been otherwise.

Nobody had ever heard of him, of the body found on the little island in the midst of the Ganges. The news was false, or else the city wasn't Benares. "Calcutta perhaps," the official said in almost incomprehensible Indian-English. "In Calcutta there's the Embassy."

We went back to the hotel. At the thought that Luca's body hadn't been found, Virginia seemed to change her mood. She became almost jolly and, as always, I felt a kind of anger. She didn't talk to me of Luca, she hadn't talked about him for years, least of all with me; but she chatted all evening, until late, stretched out in a wicker chair in the garden.

She told me only trivial details, nothing important, of her journey in India and Ladahk, ten years before . . . the color of the camels, of the Moslems' eyes, the hum of the rickshaw's wheels, the form of the seashells in the Bay of Bengal, and her amazement when, outside the great stupa of Swaiambu, Luca vanished with a German girl, a tourist he had encountered there by chance. Perhaps it was that episode, one of many, that brought things between them to a definite end. They broke up a few weeks after their return to Rome. He went off to New York for a year, to teach, and she, quite unexpectedly, came to live with me. Their house remained uninhabited and dusty: only the plants on the terrace continued to flourish, thanks to the good offices of the concierge.

During those six months when Virginia lived with me, for the first time we told each other everything. Everything . . .

what might that mean? She showed me Luca's letters and I, to wound her, showed her mine. For a few days we feigned indifference, but afterwards the indifference towards Luca became real, and the friendship between us became even more real. It was an old friendship, as I said, dating from childhood, but not a smooth friendship. The social differences, the vagueness of Virginia's moods, aroused in me an envy and an aggressiveness suppressed in long silences and fits of disaffection. But we were friends in a fatal way: I like to use this word, especially in the light of what was to happen a long, long time later.

We telephoned the Italian Embassy in Calcutta, but to no avail. They apparently knew nothing either. They told us to come there, to see if some investigation could be made. We had to wait two days before we could find seats on the plane, and in the meanwhile we pretended to be casual tourists. We went to see the bodies of the dead cremated on the steps of the Ganges. During the night, from the boat, the pyres could be seen burning, dozens and dozens at once, then the bodies stretched out one next to the other, wrapped in violet-colored saris, greased with butter, with a banana leaf between the lips. We also saw bodies of children and of sadhus floating with the current, in a peaceful indifference, slow as the course of the river, with no more ties or distinctions between life and death. That slowness had overwhelmed Luca, making him almost unable to speak, on his return from that first trip. When we made love, the very evening of his return, he was quiet beneath me, caressing me like an animal, not speaking, his eyes empty. "It's the slowness that consumes you," he said. "A magnificent sensation. Colors stop, the sky, the trees. Everything claims its right to last forever, not to be consumed. But we are the ones who consume ourselves, looking, as if we were the only corruptible and impure thing on this earth."

I had brought with me the ivory bracelet he gave me that evening, after a furious quarrel during which he had hardly

defended himself. The bracelet had been shattered, and a
year later I got it back, fastened by three silver rings which
gave it a barbaric aspect. I wore it around my wrist, and it
seemed to me the only thing of Luca still alive. Then, after
that evening, as Virginia became more talkative, time seemed
to slow down also for me, as it was invaded by a white, uniform hue, like Indian dress.

Calcutta was flooded by the monsoon. The taxi had a hard
time moving along the vast avenue, flanked by the tropical
forest dripping streams of water. The heat was oppressive. At
the Embassy they told us no foreigner had been reported
dead for at least two months. The newspaper item unques-
tionably had been false. We no longer knew what to do. We
tried telephoning Rome, but in vain. We sent telegrams to
some friends, asking them to check. We waited a few days
before going back to Benares. Virginia seemed happy, inexplicably. At intervals, interrupting her tales of previous trips
(and this narration, to me, seemed to belong to a strange region that was neither present nor past), she convinced me
that we should continue on our own, towards the South, to
Puri, Trivandium, or else to the North, to Nepal . . . Katmandu, Pokhara.

"What about Luca?" I asked.

"Luca's gone. Can't you understand that? It's a joke. A
joke, but this time we won't see him again."

She was convinced the story had been sent to the newspapers by Luca in person. But to what end? To make us rush
to him? Why wasn't he showing himself? And besides, Luca
had never had any passion for macabre jokes. Death fascinated him and repelled him, but in any case he never joked
about it. "You have to earn your death," he used to say. He
had this idea that everything had to be earned, that is, deserved, but also expiated, like an unknown sin, or a sin
difficult to confess.

And so, as we found ourselves living in our search for

Luca, we seemed to be living in an old Antonioni film, with one difference: as the days gradually passed, Luca's presence became more and more remote, and I also began to believe it a cheap joke, in bad taste, even if it was hard for me to reconcile these qualities with my idea of Luca. It seemed to me, indeed, that this journey to India was a strange test, a risk, underlined by the fact that Luca had set off alone for the first time in his life. He liked to travel with another person, preferably a woman, but also a casual friend: someone, however, who knew how to listen. "Solitary emotions are lost emotions," he would say when he happened to discover something unexpected in my company. And he must have repeated this remark to everyone, Virginia included.

This, as I said, was the first of Luca's jokes. The second came in Calcutta, at the Nepalese Embassy.

Virginia had persuaded me to go to Katmandu. "As long as we're out here, we ought to take advantage and travel around a bit. In Nepal it doesn't rain so much, and we can spend a few peaceful days at the foot of the Himalayas."

While we were waiting our turn to hand over documents and photographs, the official with Mongol features asked us our names. Then, after checking our passports, he handed us an envelope. Our names were on it, mine and Virginia's. We asked for further information, but the official seemed unwilling to understand another word of English. It's not the usual thing to leave messages for strangers at an Embassy.

It was a letter, and a meaningless one, into the bargain. Or rather, a repetition of the two letters Luca had already left us. Instructions in the event of his death: cremation, bay leaves from the Palatine, scattering of ashes in the Ganges. At the end, there was some doggerel I don't remember now. (All of Luca's letters disappeared, a few years ago, when our house, mine and Virginia's, was robbed. They were in a metal box along with some jewels of no great value. Without stopping to examine the contents, the thieves carried off the whole thing.) It seems to me that, among the rather halting verses, Luca recommended to us a little city called Muzzaffar, almost on the Nepal border.

From Muzzaffar we could continue to Katmandu by bus, a twenty-hour trip, murderous but splendid, through the forest and up among the Himalayan foothills. It was Virginia who first became enthusiastic about the bus trip, in her curiosity to rediscover something of Luca.

In one night, by train, we reached Muzzaffar. We were in high spirits and by now the journey was beginning to grip us, an adventure that chiefly concerned the two of us, while Luca became a pretext to talk about something else.

In Muzzaffar, we asked for a room in the Hotel Asia, run by Sikhs, very clean, with red turbans and curly beards and hair. "Asia" was a word in the doggerel. One of the Sikhs, after bringing us two bottles of whisky, began to speak of Luca. The description of his face, his clothes, his speech was perfect.

Luca had stayed at the Hotel Asia a week, almost never leaving his room. He had sent many letters to Europe and had said he was waiting for two women from Italy. Had he been alone? Yes, alone. When had he gone? About a month ago. Where to? Where to?

The Sikh wasn't sure of Luca's destination. He hadn't said anything, but Muzzaffar was a small city and the Sikhs know everything about the foreigners. He had left for Katmandu, by bus. Or perhaps for Benares. The man remembered Luca had said "Vharanashy," the real Hindu name for Benares.

Now we could choose: turn back, to the city where nobody would be able to give us fresh news, or else press on. It was more in the spirit of Luca to continue by bus, even if the journey wasn't a great adventure. Dozens of students, with sleeping bags, made the trip every day. It was the cheapest way to get into Nepal. And also the most uncomfortable.

Virginia soon felt ill, after three hours of traveling. I had an attack of sinusitis during the night. We stopped in a remote village, without electricity and without hotels. They put us up in a room, behind a curtain. On the other side of it, a whole Indian family was sleeping, with babies and animals. The next morning, not having closed our eyes, we paid the family a few rupees and got into the bus again. The forests were thick: on either side of the bus, which was coming apart, cliffs fell away, more and more dizzying.

Some kids were traveling on the roof and our slow progress allowed them to light an occasional joint and enjoy the landscape, stretched out under the sky of an incredible blue.

Even though we were going to Nepal in search of Luca, it was during that same journey that Luca abandoned us completely. Virginia was sleeping with her head on my shoulder, and I was stroking her hair, almost without realizing it, without thinking, in a state of bliss that the jolts of the bus were unable to disturb. The passengers, almost all Westerners, seemed caught up in a light, collective euphoria. They sang Hindu dirges, not knowing the words, and the few Indians looked at them without expression, asking them from time to time for a cigarette or an apple.

The stops were endless, but finally, at a tight curve, filled with mountain fog, the Katmandu highland opened before us, illuminated by the sun, in the midst of very green hills, with golden roofs and streets turned scarlet by the expanse of red peppers set out to dry on the ground cluttered with people, animals, and excrement all mixed together, the most authentic odor of the Orient. An odor (better not laugh) that in the long run becomes almost narcotic.

In Katmandu, from a tourist pamphlet we picked an isolated hotel. A villa with a park, dirt cheap. We hired some bicycles and rode around all day until we sank, exhausted, into a Chinese restaurant, filled with Italians drawing on their joints, like babies on their bottles.

Nepalese got up in Western style, with huge heels and fluorescent neckties, offered opium and ganja to delighted Japanese or Australian girls, disappearing then into the bedrooms of the restaurant-hotel. For the first time, Virginia took my hand and, with a completely natural movement, kissed it. I must make one thing clear, not for moralistic reasons but because I realize that, at this point, everything might seem to point towards a story quite different from ours. We never had a lesbian relationship: it wasn't necessary, if that is how to put it . . . It's a bit idiotic to have to spell out this business. There should also be a definition of friendship, which is by nature an absurdity.

Friendship isn't an abstract concept; it's a concrete emotion and, like any emotion, it is based on facts, episodes, occasions, desires, hates, impulses. In friendship, especially in a friendship that lasts a whole lifetime, all the discussions of the unconscious can duly be trotted out, but they won't achieve any big results. There has never been anything more vital, more necessary, and more contradictory than the friendship between me and Virginia. Sex was something remote, that we had perhaps experienced, separately, both of us, with Luca. No sublimations, however; only the idea that Luca had defrauded us out of some of our reciprocal feelings. As if he had absorbed them.

So our mature feelings we discovered in Nepal, in the days when Luca's traces became more and more evident, fresh. And the signs of him gradually increased, first imperceptible, then clear, very clear, like a trail already conceived and arranged for us, and also as if what was growing between me and Virginia or between Virginia and me were a prearrangement, or rather a "restitution" of what he had taken from us, in loving us or making himself loved.

If there was a plan in these traces, then that meant Luca really was disappearing and also, in some way, his love could no longer be divided between the two of us, but was joining ours.

These mingled loves were the very thing that I and Virginia had rejected firmly or, at least, vigorously. One woman's or no woman's, to echo a Pirandello title. Pirandello was also a favorite of Luca's.

This feeling, not new and yet totally new, that was being born between me and Virginia on the seat of the rickety bus and that was to continue in the Chinese restaurant in Katmandu, when both of us were dressed up as Indian tourists in cheap silk and Tibetan coats, outstripped the very plan that, perhaps, Luca had prearranged for us. A plan that, though it proceeded according to his intentions and was tinged with the darkest presentiments, preserved the slightly embarrassed enthusiasm of a discovery of adulthood.

In the evening we roamed among the temples, inhabited by a tribe of smokers and sniffers, hidden behind dark glasses or lost in the chanting of the Buddhist celebrants, their cymbals and voices attuned to the notes of the frogs. We wandered almost always hand in hand, trying not to mix with the too many Italians who crowded the big square and the little side streets. That was the first evening we really slept together. Virginia was keyed up and had forgotten all the details of her previous journeys. She seemed to live in the present, for the first time since we left home. A long driveway led to the hotel, flanked by black, leafy, aromatic trees. Virginia had taken off her sandals and was dancing with imperceptible movements under the shadow of the boughs, whistling a little song I had a hard time recognizing. Then she said: "I've grown my first white hairs. Aren't you sorry?"

"Why do you ask?"

"We've known each other so long. This white hair is evidence: don't you think?"

"We should try not to age."

"Oh, no! We must try to age like everybody else. If we don't find Luca . . ."

"What does Luca have to do with it?"

"I think he wasn't joking."

"He has been so far."

"He did it so we would come here, to collect him."

"And even if we find him, what will change?"

"Everything will change."

"Everything?"

"Everything will go back to what it was before."

"What changes then, if everything remains as it was?"

"We won't be able to age like everybody else, you and I."

"What do you think could prevent us?"

"Luca."

"I don't believe he has this power."

"He does, and you know it. If we find him, we'll end up not seeing each other anymore, or we'll see each other pointlessly, as we always did."

"Then you'd rather leave without looking for him?"

"No, that would disgust me. It would be running away. No, I want to hunt for him, but I hope he won't let himself be found. Or else, I hope he wasn't joking."

"And if you're right, what should we do?"

"Go home alone, you and I, with our hair finally gray."

"It doesn't seem a great prospect to me, this premature aging."

"It's not premature, if you choose something that makes us live forever."

"I don't understand what you mean."

"You know it as well as I do."

"What am I supposed to know?"

"That we mustn't go back to Rome with Luca. You know very well that we should remain alone, you and me, without having to share ourselves anymore with anyone."

"Does that seem something possible to you?"

"It seems to me the only truly desirable thing that we can do."

"Doesn't it seem to you that, again, we would be following Luca's wishes? We'd be doing it only because he's disappeared, as if he had been our master."

"But we have to decide now, at once, tonight . . . we mustn't wait even till tomorrow. Whether Luca is still here or isn't, nothing should change for us."

Now that Virginia had spoken, and spoken clearly, the whole inadequately expressed enchantment of those last few days became a remote and hardly real sensation. Virginia thought my same thoughts, she communicated through my same words and my same fears. I should have hugged her and clung to her, as the only really alive person in the world, the only one who could make me live beyond Luca and beyond time, which soon would age us without deceit. Instead I remained still, not speaking. Among the black branches, the lunar glow made a kind of dancing halo. There were no stars. The line of the mountains was opaque, like a damp soot that the monsoon thrust forward. An abrupt wind shook the leaves.

"I don't know," I said, starting to walk hurriedly again. "I've never thought about it. Why shouldn't we live together? We could see each other: everyone has a right to his own life. This way, it would be burying ourselves alive. It's a bit early, don't you think? If Luca really is gone (I loathed saying "dead"), we mustn't behave as if we had to flee before life. I loved him, you know that, and maybe I love him still, but I'm not an idolater."

As I spoke, taking short puffs on my cigarette, I felt I was lying, and the light shadow of Virginia beside me really seemed the only living thing I had; and yet I felt a strange fear, as if, to move closer to her, I had to close off all the world behind me and descend into the depths, in the darkness. What did I know of Virginia? Everything, absolutely everything that had happened to her in her life, but just now, as I held her hand, I felt that she was a perfect stranger to me, and I to her.

One thing, still, I couldn't deny. The incredible tenderness and security that this frail creature gave me, as she almost stammered, uncertain, at my side, in the shadows. And anyway, Luca was far off, very far, as if he had been dead for a hundred years and before those hundred years had never lived, but had only been imagined, like a fantasy among little girls who mingle desires with faces, impulses with fears, hopes with models borrowed from edifying tales or from advertising.

That very tenderness that opened before us the prospect of an unexpected familiarity decided me to continue the search for Luca, our man (to use the vocabulary I was accustomed to use in the ladies' magazine for which I had been writing for ten years). It was a nice story for those housewife readers, but now it was coming true. How the banal becomes hard, fascinating, and scary when you actually touch it. Life, as far as originality is concerned, is very disappointing.

Luca was gone and Virginia had come back. I kept thinking in these very terms: come back. And from a remote place, from an almost impossible rescue, balanced between our graying hair and a childhood of which only some photographs remained intact, but faded.

Luca was gone? Had it happened only inside us or was he really gone, in the sense that he was no longer alive? After all, what reasons did Luca have to disappear or to die? He had talked about it all his life; you could say that in his books he had never mentioned anything but that fascinating, enigmatic, and dark situation that lured him with faces always changing, always feminine. Women, sex, relationships: everything for Luca inevitably signified an attraction so morbid that it led him towards the image of an inevitable loss. And what was this loss if not the tireless imagination, the fervid energy that allowed him to desire everything, to want always what the impulse of the moment proposed to him?

Luca's intelligence, even Luca's genius, glossed over things; he never succeeded in really knowing them, and in this way he was unable to give a true identity even to himself. He often used to say so: "Each one of us receives an identity

from the things that are outside him. Alone we are nothing."
And so Luca for the whole extent of his life had never been
anyone, only a probe, an always alert eye which dismissed
from him anything that did not have the vague smell of the
end, of destruction. Hadn't he written that every work of art
uses the reason to declare something against reason? That it
uses unhappiness and sorrow to depict happiness and joy?
That without sorrow no artist could permit himself the luxury of thinking about happiness? That without sorrow everything is futile and trite? That every artist has the moral
duty to procure sorrow for himself as others procure drugs?
There was a lot of Kafka in all this, but the models, this time,
didn't count, because Luca was telling the truth.

In fact, whether through his wish or through chance, his
life was a fairly linear succession of tragic, irrevocable events.
Irreparable, indeed, as he would say. "Everything that happens is true, but precisely because it's true, it is also irreparable." To repair what has happened, to establish what power is
given man to defeat his own destiny: this was the meaning
found in his books and also in the way of life he had chosen.
But us? Virginia and I were not the irreparable, but rather
the other face of sorrow. And yet we were not enough, in
any moment, with any act, with any word. Sorrow, the
search, often selfish and false, for sorrow, the silent display of
this suffering irritated us and repelled us. Luca wanted sympathy, and his histrionic aspect was a part also of his passion
for the theater. A passion which was also irrevocable, which
had led him into acting at the age of sixteen. He had never
forgotten that experience afterwards. The theater: "place of
unlimited power, of transformations that leave everything the
same," he would sneer, provokingly. I believe he acted always: infinite goodness and gratuitous cruelty, unrestrained
eroticism, sexual ambiguity, passion. What was there in this
that was true for us, who wanted everything true, simple
and, in our way, pure? Happy feelings, a balanced existence.

What attracted us in Luca? It was Virginia who talked about it, for the first time in her life, the first night that we slept in Katmandu, amid the stifled laughter of the tourists who filled the hotel, and the slightly comic rhythm of the Tibetan dances in the garden.

Luca was false, Virginia murmured. However, that falsity had a natural, inner strength, as the reverse of the truth. And it led him to perform irreparable exploits. That falsity hid the true face of Luca, it was a little demon that never abandoned him. It was the road or the medium that he had chosen for finding something true without being frightened by it. A screen, in other words, a defense.

Finding something true . . . Had there ever been anything more lonely, egoistic, and even barren? Only what you feel, intimate and private, assumes some value. A private dialogue between the self and that enigmatic entity which can be given countless names, God, eternity, purity, truth . . . But all this, for us or for anyone else, is only a privation, an impossibility of communicating. A renunciation of being what we are or of becoming what we are. A woman who loves a man devoted to himself and articulated in an invincible pretense must renounce living: it is only a thing, a pretext, perhaps a pretext of love, but completely without emotions and impulses.

At the poles of this life Virginia and I were placed, knowing each other very well, but pretending, on our part, to know nothing now, being content with an exchange of jealousies and mute regrets.

Luca, in all of it, seemed to find pleasure and stimulation, instead of releasing that hateful immobility of feelings with which, despite ourselves, he kept us bound.

I believe we both felt quite a strong hatred for him, for that little demon so vital and true that made him unique. There were other men we knew better than him! Others who could have given us so much in those years (not many, to tell the truth) during which we were to contend for him as a unique, precious possession! Now, when Luca's enigmatic game was about to reveal his true face, exalting us in the most perfect solitude (if he was dead) or unmasking him completely (if we found him alive and well), now Virginia and I felt that this dark power had worked like a termite inside us, eliminating barriers and exploding that somewhat phony youthful friendship that had kept us close for such a long time.

Halfway through the night, the monsoon burst like fireworks. Water poured in through the shutters and from the ceiling, flooding the mats, wetting our luggage. We covered ourselves with a blanket, spread over the bed, which we had dragged to a protected corner. And under the blanket, like the two little girls of almost a lifetime earlier, we went on holding hands, unable to stop laughing at this situation, idiotic but domestic and serene.

Talking about Luca meant shifting him farther and farther away. And Virginia said, with a sigh: "You want to know something? It won't make you mad? Well, I wish he had made up his mind, once and for all."

"Made up his mind to do what?"

"To end it all. He was always talking about it . . . about death, death. I want to live. I want to feel growing inside me, and also around me, all those real things that I haven't destroyed so far. Simple things, trees, objects, landscapes, sea, birds. Everything, in other words! The game we play here, on this planet. Why should I renounce it? What do I care what's beyond, if there is anything? I take this hand of yours, you see? It's warm, soft, it gives me pleasure, makes me feel safe. This blanket shelters us, we're alone, you and I, in this country full of tourists, but also deserted and distant. You and I are the only beings, here, who can talk to each other without lying, without having to explain. Doesn't it seem magnificent to you?"

Then, inexplicably, Virginia burst into tears. Not sorrowful tears, but like a dam suddenly shattered. A river of tears that finally wet us like a tiny monsoon, that delivered us from the heat, from the drought that, little by little, kills. I, too, who was jealous of those tears, tried to make a drop or two well up, but without success. Then I put my lips to Virginia's cheeks and kissed her, and this time my desire was to taste how much life, simply carnal life, there was in those tears. Virginia held me tight.

"He's gone, I'm sure of it," she murmured. "I can't be wrong. You'll see. Tomorrow we'll go to Pokhara: he's there!"

From Luca she had acquired this certainty that she could guess, at random, the most unlikely events. I remember one winter evening, in the mountains, after skiing all day, Luca volunteered to guess the throws of the dice of the friends staying at the hotel with us. He sat there for about half an hour in silence, while the others gambled and challenged him to guess. Then, all of a sudden, he said a number: the throw of the dice confirmed his prediction. Then he shouted another, and that one also turned up. He tried about ten times, without a single mistake, then he got up and went off to bed, chuckling. "Chance, my friends: don't joke too much with it." He had drunk a bit, and I went upstairs with him.

"How did you do it?" I asked him.

"The point is not to think. It's the Hindus' dharma. Just don't think. The nonthinker is touched by grace; or rather, *is* grace. How to succeed? The secret is so easy. Nothing is easier than an impossible thing if you don't know that it is, in fact, impossible." He fell asleep, snoring, and I had to wake him several times during the night. Then, as on so many other nights, he embraced me and held me close as if to prevent me from escaping. All his strength had become concentrated in his hands, the rest was frighteningly weak.

"Don't you feel free?" Virginia asked again, flinging away the blanket. The monsoon was over. Everything was dripping, as if a thousand fountains had started, together, trickling from the roof, the trees, the mountains. The lunar radiance spread, rapidly outlining the tops of the mountains and the nearest branches of the trees. The room had an enormous window, occupying the north wall. We had only to pull aside a curtain and the whole night offered its treasures scattered by the bewitching light of the moon.

"From Luca?" I asked, also emerging from the blanket and opening the window.

"No, not exactly from him, but from the effort of fighting him, in order to have him for a little. You remember his book? One of the first. You remember the beginning: 'When the fight starts, with its divine length . . .' It's this very length, wishing that the fight would never end, that there would never be a moment of peace, of relaxation . . ."

"No . . ." I said. "Until we've found him, I'll never feel properly free. For the present I am well only when we talk. But if you're taken with one of your silences again, then I feel that everything has to start over, from the beginning. You move too far from me. Then he intervenes again and takes my breath away. And besides, enough is enough: the way we talk, Luca sounds like a soap opera character. I believe that if he's stripped of his pretenses, he becomes once more a character, or rather a person, more fragile and frightened than us."

"You think so? Mind you, he takes pleasure—it's the only pleasure he feels—in showing himself for what he isn't. In New York last year we went to the Public Theater. There was *Othello* with Orson Welles, and on the poster he wrote a line of Iago's, the one that says: 'I am not what I am.' He said that one line was worth the whole play. True greatness was right there, true desperation: not the Moor's, but the desperation of the anonymous Iago, who hates God, the world, and all the rest. He went through the whole evening, going on and on about that sentence, rolling one joint after another, knowing they wouldn't have any effect."

I wanted to know what had happened to Virginia's love and I began calmly defending Luca.

"He's not mean," I ventured.

"No, he's generous, he gives you what he has, but this too is not genuine. Only guilt feelings function in him. Possession, the joy of living in peace: all this makes him feel like a usurper. Even writing, he told me, seems an abuse to him."

"Guilty of what?"

"Of everything, of nothing. A kind of original sin, an insatiable desire to possess everything that then turns against him, because in reality everything possessed makes him feel dirty, humiliated."

"That's not bad. You can't say he ever went to any lengths to obtain anything."

"No, but he uses his cleverness with people, especially with those who love him. Then he wants to hold on to that possession at any price. And he is even capable of making you happy, for a little while. Until he is overcome by the longing to have something else. He must have told you, too, how he feels."

"Of course. He tells everybody: like an exile. From childhood on, he's always felt he was in places where he shouldn't be. Isn't that it? But this isn't entirely negative. It shows that, perhaps, his suffering is real."

"It's a luxury, a whim, believe me. And if this whim does produce real suffering, then it's even worse. Because in the end he imposes it on others. There are many good qualities that, in some people, become completely negative."

I tried to insist: his books, they at least had a value. But Virginia wouldn't be budged. She didn't give a damn about his works. At this point in her life she wanted only simple things. "The warmth of a hand, color, even a smile from people. It's wonderful to see somebody smile. It gives a sense of eternity, peace, well-being. For me, this is what counts. And until yesterday, thanks to Luca, I thought these things were all shit."

Never, in all the years that followed that trip, did I hear Virginia so harsh and so explicit. It was a kind of frenzy of which she wanted to convince herself, by making her tone sharper. At times she would happen to speak of Luca, while we were strolling near our country house, where we went to live, in retirement, a few months after our return to Rome. She told me the most intimate things and asked nothing of me in return. She talked as if she were alone, as if she herself had changed skin and now saw those somewhat dire events as a preparation for our life together. We had become old, not elderly, but with thick gray streaks now in our hair. And the subject of our life had changed. We told each other that the idea of ending our lives together, like a pair of slightly crazy and deeply devoted sisters, had come to us already in school, when Virginia came home with me for a holiday and we exchanged our first sexual information. And then at the university, after which we lost sight of each other for quite a while. She, in the United States to study photography and a lot of other things she never put to any use, and me, married, then on magazines, the usual ones, for housewives and teenage girls. We liked all of this very much, it should have begun immediately, with our first meeting.

"Why?" I asked Virginia. And she gave me a look filled with irony, then burst out laughing. "Hmph! Does there have to be a reason?"

We started breeding dogs, hiring out saddle horses, cultivating the vegetable garden, putting up jams, making natural sweets.

A series of things characteristic of perfect housekeepers liberated by postfeminism. But it was all a game. The important thing was that, through the dark thread of Luca's life, we had found, for the first time, a very serene and happy way of spending our existence. This was the only thing that mattered.

I don't remember ever having experienced, before then, the deep calm that would come over me at sunset. Virginia would fix supper, and I would help her or would go to the village to buy something or would clean the kennel or stay in the garden. When it was dark, in the moonlight, we would eat in silence. Virginia listened to classical music, especially Mozart or Bach, and I watched television, with the audio turned off. Voices bored me, and I allowed myself to be gently hypnotized by the colored images to which I lent my own words, those that I wanted to hear spoken by those silent, constantly moving faces. Virginia's music, which wasn't only Bach and Mozart, but her personal music, the music of her presence, did the rest.

After a while we went to bed, and in fact, I don't remember ever having felt, before then, such a profound peace, as I heard her breathing grow regular, along with mine, moving off in a dream.

Not even Luca would have been able to laugh at this. His sarcasm turned to helpless rage in the face of happiness. His exile became real, because nobody is so far away as the happy person, and for him, who "was not what he was," all this was not only incomprehensible, but doubly painful because it denied any form of possession on anyone's part. At moments, before falling asleep, I would happen to think, without a sigh: "Poor Luca . . ." And it would seem to me that his whole world, bristling and dark, was like a troubled carnival booth of witches where they played with real blood, real skulls, real sorrow. But in vain: those who entered paid for their ticket, then left, whereas he had to stay there eternally, turning the cranks of his booth which could never stop.

The bus, a minibus literally falling to pieces, left for Pokhara only three days later. The rain had destroyed the road at a dangerous point. So we made some side trips from Katmandu.

First of all I wanted to see the stupa of Bodnath, a giant's head under a peaked hat with squared-off corners, which looked around, its eyes buried in plaster white and blue as the sky.

Encircling the stupa was a myriad of Tibetan shops, put up by refugees from Lhasa. I bought a strange little cap made of braids of real hair, raven hair which, by itself, was enough to make anyone look Chinese; and I, with my long eyes and tanned skin, seemed a strange Negro transplanted to the Himalayas.

Virginia was excited and laughed constantly, struck up conversations with anyone, Nepalese or Western. At times she disappeared and I would retrieve her later, seated in the shade of a Buddhist temple, with a bowl of water in her hand and a prayer book carved on bamboo canes. She seemed freed of everything, even of me.

It was there in Bodnath that she reappeared, after an hour's absence, with Kurtz, an American of indefinable age, tall, thin, with a perfectly bald head, like an ivory ball. He looked at me with an almost feverish gaze. In a sack he had necklaces and ivory statuettes that he bought up in the hills from the Tibetans and sold to tourists in Pokhara and Katmandu.

"Kurtz, my name is Kurtz," he sighed, as if that name were an intolerable burden. "Perhaps we've met already . . . in Africa, or in Rome." No, I really didn't think I had ever seen him before. He offered to guide us around the cheapest shops in Katmandu. He showed us a complete sampling of drugs—opium, hashish, mescalin, acid, hallucinative mushrooms ("delicious! so good for the digestion!")—and pipes of yak horn, chillums of carved wood, and so on, explaining their use to us and suggesting the right amount for a magnificent and harmless trip.

"You're a walking manual of drugs," I said to him.

"Why, of course!" he giggled, taking my hand. "Thirty years ago I got my doctor's degree at Harvard, with a thesis on the relation between drugs and literature. It was published. Sold fairly well."

Strange, I thought: another trick of Luca's.

Luca, too, had written a manual of the sort, but certainly

not thirty years ago. I remember him telling me that before his nothing like it existed, and you could believe him.

We went back to Katmandu together on bicycles, dodging monkeys, goats, and dogs lying in the middle of the road, which rose and fell between two unbroken lines of pink poppies.

Kurtz seemed determined not to let go of us quickly. He waited for us in the hotel lobby, or rather he waited for Virginia, because I did absolutely nothing to encourage him to stay.

As I was taking a shower, Virginia, lying on the bed, asked me what I thought of Kurtz.

"An exile," I answered, trying to get a rise out of her.

"It's true! So you realized it!"

"Realized what?"

"He knows Luca."

"Did he tell you?"

"No, but just wait. Before coming here, he must have spoken to him. He's been to Rome various times, he knows a lot of people we know. Luca must certainly have met him."

"You think it was Luca who sent him to us?"

"I don't know. It seems too complicated to me, but there must be something. Luca managed to get that message to us in Calcutta, and it's even easier to find us in Katmandu, among the foreigners who all gather in the square."

"How did you find him?"

"He was the one who found me. I have the impression he had been following us since we started."

"Then he could have said what he wants right away."

"Maybe he doesn't want anything."

"Then why is he waiting for us?"

"He hopes to make a little money by selling us ivory or opium. I don't know."

"Did you tell him we're going to Pokhara?"

"No, I'm waiting for him to speak up. If Luca's expecting

us there, Kurtz will suggest we make an excursion to the foot of Annapurna. You'll see."

"I don't understand anything of this whole game, but one thing is sure: Luca is alive and wants to tease us. I'm not going to Pokhara!"

"Oh, come on, don't be silly! We came here on purpose. If it's a joke, we'll get even with him."

"I'd tell him to go screw himself, that's all. But he won't let us find him. Wait and see."

"Are you sure?"

"How can I be sure? But I have a feeling. This business smacks of a cheap literary experiment, and we're the guinea pigs."

We took our time dressing, and it was almost dark when we came upon Kurtz in the hotel lobby, calm, his eyes half closed, a now cold cup of tea in his hand. The waiting seemed to have made him even more polite and considerate. I noticed that he no longer had the little bag with the ivory items over his shoulder. When I asked him what had happened to it, he held out his arms and raised his eyes to heaven: "Sold! Everything sold!" And he showed me a handful of dollars.

"It's a fortune," he said, smiling. "Tomorrow I can come with you to Pokhara."

"With us? There's no bus tomorrow. The road is blocked."

"Not anymore, not anymore," Kurtz said, with a knowing air. "Here in Nepal everything is repaired quickly, or else it is never repaired again. Tomorrow the buses will leave as usual."

"And how do you know we're going to Pokhara?"

"It's an obligatory excursion. Don't you want to see the Himalayas?"

"Are you sure we'll go tomorrow?"

"Virginia seemed sure to me."

I looked at Virginia angrily. I felt now that I was in the center of a plot, alone. Something was being kept hidden from me. "I'm not coming," I said, with too much self-confidence. "I want to see the environs of Katmandu, and then I'm going back to Delhi. I've reserved a seat on the plane."

"Oh, really!" Virginia cried, laughing. "Don't be mad. I did tell him we might go to Pokhara with him, but we're not obliged to. If you'd rather, we can stay here. I challenged him, Mr. Kurtz: that's all."

"Challenged him to what?"

"To tell us what Luca wants of us. In fact, Kurtz, tell us right now: What does our dear Luca want of us? And don't tell me you don't know him . . ."

"I won't deny that. I don't know him very well, but he isn't a stranger to me either."

"Then, why are you sticking to us?" I asked, in a fury. "You've sold your ivory. We're not interested in drugs. What's keeping you here? Are you supposed to report to Luca what we're doing? Those dollars you just showed us— are they from Luca?"

"No, I'm not a spy." Kurtz chuckled. "Here, in Katmandu, it's easy to make friends, among Westerners. Nothing wrong, nothing underhand. A joint, an excursion, then goodbye. If you like, I'll leave at once. I didn't realize I was so unwelcome. I apologize."

"That's not it," I said, somewhat more conciliatory. "It's not your fault. But this game has gone on long enough. Tomorrow we'll come with you to Pokhara, but you must promise us we'll find Luca the moment we arrive."

"I can't be sure of that. I know he left for Pokhara a few days ago, a week perhaps. There aren't many other places around there. You can go on into Tibet on foot, but only the Nepalese know the road. It's too difficult for us."

"Then Luca is still there," Virginia said confidently.

"We'll leave tomorrow morning at six. Let's not discuss it anymore this evening."

We ate as usual in the Chinese restaurant and we went to bed early. At dawn Virginia was already awake, her luggage packed, on the bed. I dressed quickly, and we found Kurtz, with a canvas sack and a big straw hat, waiting outside the bus station. We took our seats and for eight hours we were jolted over unpaved roads, besieged by thick vegetation, with swirling rivers and inaccessible shores (maybe it was only one river, but with endless curves that multiplied it).

The bus made a number of stops. We ate the pink bananas children were selling, and nothing else. Finally we began to descend towards a valley of brilliant colors. It was cool. The Himalayas couldn't be seen. Strange, umbrella-like trees dotted the conical hills, a dark green, scattered with yellow and blue flowers, dazzling in their intensity.

At a checkpoint we had to get out, hand over our passports and wait. Pokhara could be glimpsed a kilometer away.

It was a cluster of decrepit houses, assembled in a completely random fashion. We disembarked in the midst of dust and chickens. A swarm of doddering taxis approached the tourists, and a minute later nobody was left in the dirt square.

Our taxi entered a genuine forest, with broad patches of shade. At intervals, the roof of a colonial-style villa emerged from the green, giving a sensation of peace, oblivious of everything.

"Hotel Stavrogin," Kurtz said promptly. "You can trust it. It's not expensive and has an enviable location."

"Have you been there before?" Virginia asked.

"Of course."

"Luca too?"

"I think so. It's a hotel for Western tourists. It's particularly crowded in winter, when people go off trekking into the mountains; but it's pleasant in summer as well, and properly equipped."

This trivial conversation irked me. What did the hotel matter? We hadn't come here as tourists. Was Luca here or wasn't he? My voice turned shrill. Something was making me violently emotional, and the more I strove to control myself, the more that emotion made my heart pound. At the appearance of the lake, a splendid lake with a tiny island in its center, a deep sadness colored the whole landscape, everything I could manage to see. The sky was clear, only an occasional cloud writhed halfway up the mountains which, for this reason, did not reveal their height. Everything was very green and damp, and to me those colors seemed a funereal signal, a message written on everything, alive or inanimate. Virginia seemed unaware of it all, she talked with Kurtz, laughed with a completely natural gaiety. Was I, then, the only one thinking of Luca? Wasn't this the place we were looking for? Wasn't Luca the reason for our journey? I thought of the first evening in Katmandu, the trip from Muzzaffar . . . yes, perhaps our goal, at this point, was something else. We had to accomplish, formally, what we had been impelled to do at the beginning. No more.

Kurtz paid the driver and asked the clerk of the Stavrogin for two rooms. The hotel really was very beautiful. Little wooden bungalows, dispersed in the forest, with trimmed lawns. An enormous bath with shower, the likes of which we hadn't seen since leaving home. Everything, however, was immobile, glacial. Even the stage setting of that hotel for lovers seemed not to have been chosen by accident. Since there was no love in me anymore, or in Virginia, that place seemed to take on an ironic or even sarcastic meaning. We spent the morning walking in the woods civilized by paths filled with ivory or gilded silver alloy objects, woolen stuffs with stupendous colors. We bought a bit of everything, but a little before noon, when we were about to come back for lunch, a boy, tiny and muscular, urged us insistently to hire his boat for an excursion to the little island. There was a beautiful Buddhist temple there, and the boy seemed on the verge of tears at our determined refusal. Then Virginia took me by the hand and led me towards the boat. The lugubrious sensation gripped my throat. My eyes suddenly filled with tears.

The boat was heavy and cleaved the still waters of the lake confidently. Little white flowers dropped on our heads from the highest boughs of the trees and collected like newly blossoming corollas on the brief waves that the prow stirred at either side of the boat. Instead of growing larger, the island, as we gradually neared it, seemed to become smaller, a surfacing of gilded sand in the midst of the murky green water.

The boy rowed almost without watching. It seemed to me, in fact, that he kept his eyes shut or half shut, completely indifferent to what was happening.

We stepped out, barefoot, into the water. We sank into soft mud up to our ankles. The temple was in ruins. A reed shed protected the gilded image of the goddess Kannon. Behind her, a peeling fresco showed traces of blue and red, a dragon with bulging eyes.

There was a pile of rags just to the side of the shed, a disemboweled animal or a random heap of stones.

Virginia let go of my hand.

"There he is," she said softly.

The boy had gone back to the boat, and for a moment I was afraid he would leave us there.

We advanced slowly, almost in disbelief that the game could end as we had dreamed it or only imagined it.

Luca was there, wrapped in a blanket streaked with red and blue.

I stopped a few paces away, as Virginia went closer and, bending over his body, pulled away the blanket. He was lying supine, as if a sudden blow had felled him. I remember only the color of his skin, a wine red, horrible, distant, inaccessible.

As we returned towards the hotel, seated in the bottom of the boat without speaking, without even asking ourselves why, the clouds that covered the peaks of Annapurna were stirred by an impetuous wind and the whole chain appeared wondrously, peaks of a transparent, crystalline vertigo. The moon appeared like a premature summons, exactly opposite the sun. Then the monsoon unleashed a river of water on everything.

Virginia is picking tomatoes in the garden. I have finished writing this belated memoir, and I am wondering why. Thirty years have gone by, and we are old. We have always lived here, in Virginia's country house, never moving from that ancient place which has kept every unpleasant event far from us.

Our life is repeated, the same, every day, and this repetition is the inexhaustible source of our tranquil happiness. We haven't spoken of Luca again, and, if it weren't for these pages, I believe we wouldn't even remember him anymore.

This desire that seized me (a desire that will not recur, that's sure) is so strange that I wonder if I have really written all these words.

THE QUILT MAKER

Angela Carter

ANGELA CARTER *was born in 1940 and lives in London. She has published seven novels, including* The Passion of New Eve *(1977);* two collections of short stories, the most recent of which is The Bloody Chamber *(1979); and a feminist monograph on the Marquis de Sade,* The Sadean Woman *(1979). Her work has been translated into most European languages.*

THE QUILT MAKER
by Angela Carter

One theory is, we make our destinies like blind men chucking paint at a wall; we never understand nor even see the marks we leave behind us. But not too much of the grandly accidental abstract expressionist about *my* life, I trust; oh, no. I always try to live on the best possible terms with my unconscious and let my right hand know what my left is doing and, fresh every morning, scrutinize my dreams. Abandon, therefore, or, rather, deconstruct the blind-action painter metaphor; take it apart, formalize it, put it together again, strive for something a touch more hard-edged, intentional, altogether less arty, for I do believe that we all have the right to choose.

In patchwork, a neglected household art—neglected, obviously, because my sex excelled in it—well, there you are; that's the way it's been, isn't it? Not that I've anything against fine art, mind; nevertheless, it took a hundred years for fine artists to catch up with the kind of brilliant abstraction that any ordinary housewife used to be able to put together in only a year, five years, ten years, without making a song and dance about it.

However, in patchwork, an infinitely flexible yet harmonious overall design is kept in the head and worked out in whatever material happens to turn up in the ragbag: party frocks, sackcloth, pieces of wedding dress, of shroud, of bandage, dress shirts etc. Things that have been worn out or torn, remnants, bits and pieces left over from making blouses. One may appliqué upon one's patchwork birds, fruit and flowers that have been clipped out of glazed chintz left over from covering armchairs or making curtains, and do all manner of things with this and that.

The final design is indeed modified by the availability of materials; but not, necessarily, much.

For the paper patterns from which she snipped out regular rectangles and hexagons of cloth, the thrifty housewife often used up old love letters.

With all patchwork, you must start in the middle and work outward, even in the kind they call "crazy patchwork," which is made by feather-stitching together arbitrary shapes scissored out at the maker's whim.

Patience is a great quality in the maker of patchwork.

The more I think about it, the more I like this metaphor. You can really make this image work for its living; it synthesizes perfectly both the miscellany of experience and the use we make of it.

Born and bred as I was in the Protestant north working-class tradition, I am also pleased with the metaphor's overtones of thrift and hard work.

Patchwork. Good.

Somewhere along my thirtieth year to heaven—a decade ago now—I was in the Greyhound Bus Station in Houston, Texas, with a man I was then married to. He gave me an American coin of small denomination (he used to carry about all our money for us because he did not trust me with it). Individual compartments in a large vending machine in this bus station contained various cellophane-wrapped sandwiches, biscuits and candy bars. There was a compartment with two peaches in it, rough-cheeked Dixie Reds that looked like Victorian pincushions. One peach was big. The other peach was small. I conscientiously selected the smaller peach.

"Why did you do that?" asked the man to whom I was married.

"Somebody else might want the big peach," I said.

"What's that to you?" he said.

I date my moral deterioration from this point.

No; honestly. Don't you see, from this peach story, how I was brought up? It wasn't—truly it wasn't—that I didn't think I deserved the big peach. Far from it. What it was, was that all my basic training, all my internalized values, told me to leave the big peach there for somebody who wanted it more than I did.

Wanted it; desire, more imperious by far than need. I had the greatest respect for the desires of other people, although, at that time, my own desires remained a mystery to me. Age has not clarified them except in matters of the flesh, in which now I know very well what I want; and that's quite enough of that, thank you. If you're looking for true confessions of that type, take your business to another shop. Thank you.

The point of this story is, if the man who was then my husband hadn't told me I was a fool to take the little peach, then I never would have left him because, in truth, he was, in a manner of speaking, always the little peach to me.

Formerly, I had been a lavish peach thief, but I learned to take the small one because I had never been punished, as follows:

Canned fruit was a very big deal in my social class when I was a kid and during the Age of Austerity, food-rationing and so on. Sunday teatime; guests; a glass bowl of canned peach slices on the table. Everybody gossipping and milling about and, by the time my mother put the teapot on the table, I had surreptitiously contrived to put away a good third of those peaches, thieving them out of the glass bowl with my crooked forepaw the way a cat catches goldfish. I would have been—shall we say, for the sake of symmetry— ten years old; and chubby.

My mother caught me licking my sticky fingers and laughed and said I'd already had my share and wouldn't get any more, but when she filled the dishes up, I got just as much as anybody else.

I hope you understand, therefore, how, by the time two more decades had rolled away, it was perfectly natural for me to take the little peach; had I not always been loved enough to feel I had some to spare? What a dangerous state of mind I was in, then!

As any fool could have told him, my ex-husband is much happier with his new wife; as for me, there then ensued ten years of grab, grab, grab, didn't there, to make up for lost time.

Until it is like crashing a soft barrier, this collision of my internal calendar, on which dates melt like fudge, with the tender inexorability of time of which I am not, quite, yet, the ruins (although my skin fits less well than it did, my gums recede apace, I crumple like chiffon in the thigh). Forty.

The significance, the real significance, of the age of forty is that you are, along the allotted span, nearer to death than to birth. Along the lifeline I am now past the halfway mark. But, indeed, are we not ever, in some sense, past that halfway mark, because we know when we were born but we do not know . . .

So, having knocked about the four corners of the world awhile, the ex-peach thief came back to London, to the famil- iar seclusion of privet hedges and soiled lace curtains in the windows of tall, narrow terraces. Those streets that always seem to be sleeping, the secrecy of perpetual Sunday after- noons; and in the long, brick-walled back gardens, where the little town foxes who subsist off mice and garbage bark at night, there will be the soft pounce, sometimes, of an owl. The city is a thin layer on top of a wilderness that pokes through the paving stones, here and there, in tufts of grass and ragwort. Wood doves with mucky pink bosoms croon in the old trees at the bottom of the garden; we double-bar the door against burglars, but that's nothing new.

Next door's cherry is coming out again. It's April's quick-change act—one day, bare; the next, dripping its curds of bloom.

One day, once, sometime after the incident with the little peach, when I had put two oceans and a continent between myself and my ex-husband, while I was earning a Sadie Thompsonesque living as a barmaid in the Orient, I found myself, on a free weekend, riding through a flowering grove on the other side of the world with a young man who said: "Me Butterfly, you Pinkerton." And, though I denied it hotly at the time, so it proved, except, when I went away, it was for good. I never returned with an American friend, grant me sufficient good taste.

A small, moist, green wind blew the petals of the scattering cherry blossom through the open windows of the stopping train. They brushed his forehead and caught on his eyelashes and shook off onto the slatted wooden seats; we might have been a wedding party, except that we were pelted, not with confetti, but with the imagery of the beauty, the fragility, the fleetingness of the human condition.

"The blossoms always fall," he said.

"Next year, they'll come again," I said comfortably; I was a stranger here, I was not attuned to the sensibility, I believed that life was for living and not for regret.

"What's that to me?" he said.

You used to say you would never forget me. That made me feel like the cherry blossom, here today and gone tomorrow; it is not the kind of thing one says to a person with whom one proposes to spend the rest of one's life, after all. And, after all that, for three hundred and fifty-two in each leap year, I never think of you, sometimes. I cast the image into the past, like a fishing line, and up it comes with a gold mask on the hook, a mask with real tears at the ends of its eyes, but tears which are no longer anybody's tears.

Time has drifted over your face.

The cherry tree in next-door's garden is forty feet high, tall as the house, and it has survived many years of neglect. In fact, it has not one but two tricks up its arboreal sleeve; each trick involves three sets of transformations and these it performs regularly as clockwork each year, the first in early, the second in late spring. Thus:

one day, in April, sticks; the day after, flowers; the third day, leaves. Then—

through May and early June, the cherries form and ripen until, one fine day, they are rosy and the birds come, the tree turns into a busy tower of birds admired by a tranced circle of cats below. (We are a neighborhood rich in cats.) The day after, the tree bears nothing but cherry pits picked perfectly clean by quick, clever beaks, a stone tree.

The cherry is the principal monument of Letty's wild garden. How wonderfully unattended her garden grows all the soft months of the year, from April through September! Dandelions come before the swallow does and languorously blow away in drifts of fuzzy seed. Then up sprouts a long bolster of creeping buttercups. After that, bindweed distributes its white cornets everywhere, it climbs over everything in Letty's garden, it swarms up the concrete post that sustains the clothesline on which the lady who lives in the flat above Letty hangs her underclothes out to dry, by means of a pulley from her upstairs kitchen window. She never goes into the garden. She and Letty have not been on speaking terms for twenty years.

I don't know why Letty and the lady upstairs fell out

twenty years ago, when the latter was younger than I, but Letty already an old woman. Now Letty is almost blind and almost deaf but, all the same, enjoys, I think, the changing colors of this disorder, the kaleidoscope of the seasons variegating the garden that neither she nor her late brother have touched since the war, perhaps for some now forgotten reason, perhaps for no reason.

Letty lives in the basement with her cat.

Correction. Used to live.

Oh, the salty realism with which the Middle Ages put skeletons on gravestones, with the motto: "As I am now, so ye will be!" The birds will come and peck us bare.

I heard a dreadful wailing coming through the wall in the middle of the night. It could have been either of them, Letty or the lady upstairs, pissed out of their minds, perhaps, letting it all hang out, shrieking and howling, alone, driven demented by the heavy anonymous London silence of the fox-haunted night. I put my ear nervously to the wall to seek the source of the sound. "Help!" said Letty in the basement. The cow that lives upstairs later claimed she never heard a cheep, tucked up under the eaves in dreamland sleep while I leaned on the doorbell for twenty minutes, seeking to rouse her. Letty went on calling: "Help!" Then I telephoned the police, who came flashing lights, wailing sirens, and double-parked dramatically, leaping out of the car, leaving the doors swinging; emergency call.

But they were wonderful. Wonderful. (We're not black, any of us, of course.) First, they tried the basement door, but it was bolted on the inside as a precaution against burglars. Then they tried to force the front door, but it wouldn't budge, so they smashed the glass in the front door and unfastened the catch from the inside. But Letty, for fear of burglars, had locked herself securely in her basement bedroom, and her voice floated up the stairs: "Help!"

So they battered her bedroom door open too, splintering the door jamb, making a terrible mess. The cow upstairs, mind, sleeping sweetly throughout, or so she later claimed. Letty had fallen out of bed, bringing the bedclothes with her, knotting herself up in blankets, in a gray sheet, an old patch-work bedcover lightly streaked at one edge with dried shit, and she hadn't been able to pick herself up again, had lain in a helpless tangle on the floor calling for help until the coppers came and scooped her up and tucked her in and made all cozy. She wasn't surprised to see the police; hadn't she been calling: "Help"? Hadn't help come?

"How old are you, love," the coppers said. Deaf as she is, she heard the question, the geriatric's customary trigger.

"Eighty," she said. Her age is the last thing she has left to be proud of. (See how, with age, one defines oneself by age, as one did in childhood.)

Think of a number. Ten. Double it. Twenty. Add ten again. Thirty. And again. Forty. Double that. Eighty. If you reverse this image, you obtain something like those Russian nests of wooden dolls, in which big babushka contains a middling babushka who contains a small babushka who contains a tiny babushka and so on *ad infinitum*.

But I am further away from the child I was, the child who stole the peaches, than I am from Letty. For one thing, the peach thief was a plump brunette; I am a skinny redhead.

Henna. I have had red hair for twenty years. (When Letty had already passed through middle age.) I first dyed my hair red when I was twenty. I freshly henna'd my hair yesterday.

Henna is a dried herb sold in the form of a scum-green-colored powder. You pour this powder into a bowl and add boiling water; you mix the powder into a paste using, say, the handle of a wooden spoon. (It is best not to let henna touch metal, or so they say.) This henna paste is no longer grayish, but now a dark and vivid green, as if the hot water had re-

vived the real color of the living leaf, and it smells deliciously
of spinach. You also add the juice of half a lemon; this is supposed to "fix" the final color. Then you rub this hot, stiff
paste into the roots of your hair.

(However did they first think of it?)

You're supposed to wear rubber gloves for this part of the
process, but I can never be bothered to do that, so, for the
first few days after I have refreshed my henna, my fingertips
are as if heavily nicotine-stained. Once the green mud has
been thickly applied to the hair, you wrap it in an imperme-
able substance—a polythene bag, or kitchen foil—and leave it
to cook. For one hour: auburn highlights. For three hours: a
sort of vague russet halo round the head. Six hours: red as
fire.

Mind you, henna from different *pays d'origines* has
different effects—Persian henna, Egyptian henna, Pakistani
henna, all these produce different tones of red, from that
brick red usually associated with the idea of henna to a dark,
burning, courtesan plum or cockatoo scarlet. I am a connoisseur of henna, by now, "an unpretentious henna from the
southern slope," that kind of thing. I've been every redhead
in the book. But people think I am naturally redheaded and
even make certain tempestuous allowances for me, as they
did for Rita Hayworth, who purchased red hair at the same
mythopoeic counter where Marilyn Monroe acquired her
fatal fairness. Perhaps I first started dying my hair in order to
acquire the privileged irrationality of redheads. Some men
say they adore redheads. These men usually have very interesting psychosexual problems and shouldn't be let out
without their mothers.

When I combed Letty's hair next morning, to get her
ready for the ambulance, I saw the telltale scales of henna'd
dandruff lying along her scalp, although her hair itself is now
a vague salt and pepper color and, I hazard, has not been
washed since about the time I was making the peach decision
in the Houston, Texas, bus station. At that time, I had appro-

priately fruity—tangerine-colored—hair in, I recall, a crewcut
as brutal as that of Joan of Arc at the stake—such as we
daren't risk now, oh, no. Now we need shadows, my vain
face and I; I wear my hair down to my shoulders now. At
the moment, henna produces a reddish-gold tinge on me.
That is because I am going gray.

Because the effect of henna is also modified by the real
color of the hair beneath. This is what it does to white hair:

In Turkey, in a small country town with a line of poplar
trees along the horizon and a dirt-floored square, chickens,
motorbikes, apricot sellers, and donkeys, a woman was hag-
gling for those sesame-seed-coated bracelets of bread you can
wear on your arm. From the back, she was small and slender;
she was wearing loose, dark-blue trousers in a peasant print
and a scarf wound round her head, but from beneath this
scarf there fell down the most wonderful long, thick, Rapun-
zel-like plait of golden hair. Pure gold; gold as a wedding
ring. This single plait fell almost to her feet and was as thick
as my two arms held together. I waited impatiently to see the
face of this fairy-tale creature.

Stringing her breads on her wrist, she turned; and she was
old.

"What a life," said Letty, as I combed her hair.

Of Letty's life I know nothing. I know one or two things
about her: how long she has lived in this basement—since before I was born, how she used to live with an older brother,
who looked after her, an *older* brother. That he, last November, fell off a bus, what they call a "platform accident," fell
off the platform of a moving bus when it slowed for the stop
at the bottom of the road and, falling, irreparably cracked his
head on a curbstone.

Last November, just before the platform accident, her
brother came knocking at our door to see if we could help

him with a light that did not work. The light in their flat did not work because the cable had rotted away. The landlord promised to send an electrician but the electrician never came. Letty and her brother used to pay two pounds fifty pence a week rent. From the landlord's point of view, this was not an economic rent; it would not cover his expenses on the house, rates etc. From the point of view of Letty and her late brother, this was not an economic rent, either, because they could not afford it.

Correction: Letty and her brother could not afford it because he was too proud to allow the household to avail itself of the services of the caring professions, social workers and so on. After her brother died, the caring professions visited Letty *en masse* and now her financial position is easier, her rent is paid for her.

Correction: *was* paid for her.

We know her name is Letty because she was banging about blindly in the dark kitchen as we/he looked at the fuse box and her brother said fretfully: "Letty, give over!"

What Letty once saw and heard before the fallible senses betrayed her into a world of halftones and muted sounds is unknown to me. What she touched, what moved her, are mysteries to me. She is Atlantis to me. How she earned her living, why she and her brother came here first, all the real bricks and mortar of her life have collapsed into a rubble of forgotten past.

I cannot guess what were or are her desires.

She was softly fretful herself, she said: "They're not going to take me away, are they?" Well, they won't let her stay here on her own, will they, not now she has proved that she can't be trusted to lie still in her own bed without tumbling out arse over tip in a trap of blankets, incapable of righting herself. After I combed her hair, when I brought her some tea, she asked me to fetch her porcelain teeth from a saucer on the dressing table, so that she could eat the biscuit. "Sorry about that," she said. She asked me who the person standing beside me was; it was my own reflection in the dressing-table mirror, but, all the same, oh, yes, she was in perfectly sound mind, if you stretch the definition of "sound" only a very little. One must make allowances. One will do so for oneself.

She needed to sit up to drink the tea, I lifted her. She was so frail it was like picking up a wicker basket with nothing inside it; I braced myself for a burden and there was none, she was as light as if her bones were filled with air like the bones of birds. I felt she needed weights, to keep her from floating up to the ceiling following her airy voice. Faint odor of the lion house in the bedroom and it was freezing cold, although, outside, a good deal of April sunshine and the first white flakes of cherry blossom shaking loose from the tight buds.

Letty's cat came and sat on the end of the bed. "Hello, pussy," said Letty.

One of those ill-kempt balls of fluff old ladies keep, this cat looks as if he's unraveling, its black fur has rusted and faded at the same time, but some cats are naturals for the caring professions—they will give you mute company long after anyone else has stopped tolerating your babbling, they don't judge, don't give a damn if you wet the bed and, when the eyesight fades, freely offer themselves for the consolation of still sentient fingertips. He kneads the shit-stained quilt with his paws and purrs.

The cow upstairs came down at last and denied all knowledge of last night's rumpus; she claimed she had slept so soundly she didn't hear the doorbell or the forced entry. She must have passed out or something, or else wasn't there at all but out on the town with her man friend. Or, her man friend was here with her *all the time* and she didn't want anybody to know so kept her head down. We see her man friend once or twice a week as he arrives crabwise to her door with the furtiveness of the adulterer. The cow upstairs is fiftyish, as well preserved as if she'd sprayed herself all over with the hair lacquer that keeps her bright brown curls in tight discipline.

No love lost between her and Letty. "What a health hazard! What a fire hazard!" Letty, downstairs, dreamily hallucinating in the icy basement as the cow upstairs watches me sweep up the broken glass on the hall floor. "She oughtn't to be left. She ought to be in a home." The final clincher: "For her *own good*."

Letty dreamily apostrophized the cat; they don't let cats into any old people's homes that I know of.

Then the social worker came; and the doctor; and the district nurse; and, out of nowhere, a great-niece, probably summoned by the social worker, a great-niece in her late twenties with a great-great-niece clutching a teddy bear. Letty is pleased to see the great-great-niece, and this child is the first crack that appears in the picture that I'd built up of Letty's secluded, lonely old age. We hadn't realized there were kin; indeed, the great-niece puts us in our place good and proper. "It's up to family now," she said, so we curtsy and retreat, and this great-niece is sharp as a tack, busy as a bee, proprietorial yet tender with the old lady. "Letty, what have you got up to now?" Warding us outsiders off; perhaps she is ashamed of the shit-stained quilt, the plastic bucket of piss beside Letty's bed.

As they were packing Letty's things in an airline bag the great-niece brought, the landlord—by a curious stroke of fate —chose this very day to collect Letty's rent and perked up no end, stroking his well-shaven chin, to hear the cow upstairs go on and on about how Letty could no longer cope, how she endangered property and life on the premises by forcing men to come and break down doors.

What a life.

Then the ambulance came.

Letty is going to spend a few days in hospital.

This street is, as estate agents say, rapidly improving; the lace curtains are coming down, the round paper lampshades going up like white balloons in each front room. The landlord promised the cow upstairs five thousand pounds in her hand to move out after Letty goes, so that he can renovate the house and sell it with vacant possession for a tremendous profit.

We live in hard-nosed times.

The still unravished bride, the cherry tree, takes flowering possession of the wild garden; the ex-peach thief contemplates the prospect of ripe fruit the birds will eat, not I.

Curious euphemism "to go," meaning death, to depart on a journey.

Somewhere along another year to heaven, I elicited the following laborious explanation of male sexual response, which is the other side of the moon, the absolute mystery, the one thing I can never know.

"You put it in, which isn't boring. Then you rock backwards and forwards. That can get quite boring. Then you come. That's not boring."

For "you," read "him."

"You come; or, as we Japanese say, go."

Just so. "*Ikimasu*," to go. The Japanese orgasmic departure renders the English orgasmic arrival, as if the event were reflected in a mirror and the significance of it altogether different—whatever significance it may have, that is. Desire disappears in its fulfilment, which is cold comfort for hot blood and the reason why there is no such thing as a happy ending.

Besides all this, Japanese puts all its verbs at the ends of its sentences, which helps to confuse the foreigner all the more, so it seemed to me they themselves never quite knew what they were saying half the time.

"Everything here is arsy-varsy."

"No. Where you are is arsy-varsy."

And never the twain shall meet. He loved to be bored; don't think he was contemptuously dismissive of the element of boredom inherent in sexual activity. He adored and venerated boredom. He said that dogs, for example, were never bored, nor birds, so, obviously, the capacity that distinguished man from the other higher mammals, from the scaled and feathered things, was that of boredom. The more bored one was, the more one expressed one's humanity.

He liked redheads. "Europeans are so colorful," he said.

He was a tricky bugger, that one, a Big Peach, all right; face of Gérard Philipe, soul of Nechaev. I grabbed, grabbed and grabbed and, since I did not have much experience in grabbing, often bit off more than I could chew. Exemplary fate of the plump peach-thief; someone refuses to be assimilated. Once a year, when I look at Letty's cherry tree in flower, I put the image to work, I see the petals fall on a face that looked as if it had been hammered out of gold, like the mask of Agamemnon which Schliemann found at Troy.

The mask turns into a shining carp and flips off the hook at the end of the fishing line. The one that got away.

Let me not romanticize you too much. Because what would I do if you *did* resurrect yourself? Came knocking at my door in all your foul, cool chic of designer jeans and leather blouson and your pocket stuffed with G.N.P., arriving somewhat late in the day to make an honest woman of me as you sometimes used to threaten that you might? "When you're least expecting it . . ." God, I'm forty, now. Forty! I had you marked down for a Demon Lover; what if indeed you popped up out of the grave of the heart bright as a button with an American car purring outside waiting to whisk me away to where the lilies grow on the bottom of the sea? "I am now married to a house carpenter," as the girl in the song explained hurriedly. But, all the same, off she went with the lovely cloven-footed one. But I wouldn't. Not I.

And how very inappropriate too, the language of antique ballads in which to address one who knew best the international language of the jukebox. You'd have one of those Wurlitzer Cadillacs you liked, that you envied G.I.'s for, all ready to humiliate me with; it would be bellowing out quadraphonic sound. The Everly Brothers. Jerry Lee Lewis. Early Presley. ("When I grow up," you reveried, "I'm going to Memphis to marry Presley.") You were altogether too much, you pure child of the late twentieth century, you person from the other side of the moon or mirror, and your hypothetical arrival is a catastrophe too terrifying to contemplate, even in the most plangent state of regret for one's youth.

I lead a quiet life in South London. I grind my coffee beans and drink my cup to a spot of early baroque on the radio. I am now married to a house carpenter. Like the culture that created me, I am receding into the past at the rate of knots. Soon I'll need a whole row of footnotes if anybody under thirty-five is going to comprehend the least thing I say.

And yet . . .

Going out into the back garden to pick rosemary to put inside a chicken, the daffodils in the uncut grass, enough blackbirds out to make a pie.

Letty's cat sits on Letty's windowsill. The blinds are drawn; the social worker drew them five days ago before she drove off in her little Fiat to the hospital, following Letty in the ambulance. I call to Letty's cat but he doesn't turn his head. His fluff has turned to spikes, he looks spiny as a horse-chestnut husk.

Letty is in hospital supping broth from a spouted cup and, for all my kind heart, of which I am so proud, my empathy and so on, I myself had not given Letty's companion another thought until today, going out to pick rosemary with which to stuff a roast for our greedy dinners.

I called him again. At the third call, he turned his head. His eyes looked as if milk had been poured into them. The garden wall too high to climb since now I am less limber than

I was, I chucked half the contents of a guilty tin of cat food over. Come and get it.

Letty's cat never moved, only stared at me with its curtained eyes. And then all the fat, sleek cats from every garden up and down the road twitched their noses and came jumping, leaping, creeping to the unexpected feast and gobbled all down, every crumb, quick as a wink. What a lesson for a giver of charity! At the conclusion of this heartless banquet at which I'd been the thoughtless host, the company of well-cared-for beasts stretched their swollen bellies in the sun and licked themselves, and then, at last, Letty's cat heaved up on its shaky legs and launched itself, plop, onto the grass.

I thought, perhaps he got a belated whiff of cat food and came for his share, too late, all gone. The other cats ignored him. He staggered when he landed but soon righted himself. He took no interest at all in the stains of cat food, though. He managed a few doddering steps among the dandelions. Then I thought he might be going to chew a few stems of medicinal grass; but he did not so much lower his head towards it as let his head drop, as if he had no strength left to lift it. His sides were caved-in under the stiff, voluminous fur. He had not been taking care of himself. He peered vaguely around, swaying.

You could almost have believed, not that he was waiting for the person who always fed him to come and feed him again as usual, but that he was pining for Letty herself.

Then his hind legs began to shudder involuntarily. He so convulsed himself with shuddering that his hind legs jerked off the ground; he danced. He jerked and shuddered, shuddered and jerked, until at last he vomited up a small amount of white liquid. Then he pulled himself to his feet again and lurched back to the windowsill. With a gigantic effort, he dragged himself up.

Later on, somebody jumped over the wall, more sprightly than I, and left a bowl of bread and milk. But the cat ignored that too. Next day, both were still there, untouched.

The day after that, only the bowl of sour sops, and cherry blossom petals drifting across the vacant windowsill.

Small sins of omission remind one of greater sins of omission; at least sins of commission have the excuse of choice, of intention. However:

May. A blowy, bright-blue, bright-green morning; I go out on the front steps with a shifting plastic sack of garbage and what do I see but the social worker's red Fiat putter to a halt next door.

In the hospital they'd henna'd Letty. An octogenarian redhead, my big babushka who contains my forty, my thirty, my twenty, my ten years within her fragile basket of bones, she has returned, not in a humiliating ambulance, but on her own two feet that she sets down more firmly than she did. She has put on a little weight. She has a better color, not only in her hair but in her cheeks.

The landlord, foiled.

Escorted by the social worker, the district nurse, the home help, the abrasive yet not ungentle niece, Letty is escorted down the unswept, grass-grown basement stairs into her own scarcely used front door that someone with a key has remembered to unbolt from inside for her return. Her new cockatoo crest—whoever henna'd her really understood henna—points this way and that way as she makes sure that nothing in the street has changed, even if she can see only large blocks of light and shadow, hear, not the shrieking blackbirds, but only the twitch of the voices in her ear that shout: "Carefully does it, Letty."

"I can manage," she said tetchily.

The door the policemen battered in closes upon her and her chattering entourage.

The window of the front room of the cow upstairs slams down, bang.

And what am I to make of that? I'd set it up so carefully, an enigmatic structure about evanescence and aging and the mists of time, shadows lengthening, cherry blossom, forgetting, neglect, regret . . . the sadness, the sadness of it all . . .

But. Letty. Letty came home.

In the corner shop, the cow upstairs, mad as fire: "They should have certified her"; the five grand the landlord promised her so that he could sell the house with vacant possession has blown away on the May wind that disintegrated the dandelion clocks. In Letty's garden now is the time for fierce yellow buttercups; the cherry blossom is over, no regrets.

I hope she is too old and too far gone to miss the cat.

Fat chance.

I hope she never wonders if the nice young couple next door thought of feeding him.

But she has come home to die at her own apparently ample leisure in the comfort and privacy of her basement; she has exercised, has she not, her right to choose, she has turned all this into crazy patchwork.

Somewhere along my thirtieth year, I left a husband in a bus station in Houston, Texas, a town to which I have never returned, over a quarrel about a peach which, at the time, seemed to sum up the whole question of the rights of individuals within relationships, and, indeed, perhaps it did.

As you can tell from the colorful scraps of oriental brocade and Turkish homespun I have sewn into this bedcover, I then (call me Ishmael) wandered about for a while and sowed (or sewed) a wild oat or two into this useful domestic article, this product of thrift and imagination, with which I hope to cover myself in my old age to keep my brittle bones warm. (How cold it is in Letty's basement.)

But, okay, so I always said the blossom would come back again, but Letty's return from the clean white grave of the geriatric ward is *ridiculous!* And, furthermore, when I went out into the garden to pick a few tulips, there he is, on the other side of the brick wall, lolling voluptuously among the creeping buttercups, fat as butter himself—Letty's been feeding him up.

"I'm pleased to see *you*," I said.

In a Japanese folk tale it would be the ghost of her cat, rusty and tactile as in life, the poor cat pining itself from death to life again to come to the back door at the sound of her voice. But we are in South London on a spring morning. Lorries fart and splutter along the Wandsworth Road. Capital Radio is braying from an upper window. An old cat, palpable as a second-hand fur coat, drowses among the buttercups.

We know when we were born but—

the times of our reprieves are equally random.

Shake it out and look at it again, the flowers, fruit and bright stain of henna, the Russian dolls, the wrinkling chiffon of the flesh, the old songs, the cat, the woman of eighty; the woman of forty, with dyed hair and most of her own teeth, who is *ma semblable, ma soeur*. Who now recedes into the deceptive privacy of a genre picture, a needlewoman, a quilt-maker, a middle-aged woman sewing patchwork in a city garden, turning her face vigorously against the rocks and trees of the patient wilderness waiting round us.

MY MOTHER'S NAME

("De Naam Van Mijn Moeder")

Hannes Meinkema   HANS VERMEULEN

HANNES MEINKEMA *was born in 1943 and appeared on the literary scene in 1974 with her novel* The Mooneater. *This was followed in 1975 by a collection of short stories entitled* Summer Is a Long Time in Coming. *With her third book,* And Then There'll Be Coffee (*novel, 1976*), *which became a bestseller, she became the most widely read and best-known woman author in the Netherlands. She next published another collection of short stories* The Green Widow and Other Stories (*1977*), The Inner Egg (*novel, 1979*), *and* My Mother's Name (*stories, 1980*).

MY MOTHER'S NAME

("De Naam Van Mijn Moeder")

by Hannes Meinkema

TRANSLATED FROM THE DUTCH
BY JAMES BROCKWAY

Why did I do it? Did I do it to revenge myself on her, or just to be closer to her? Am I crazy, am I sick?

After the divorce we were completely dependent on each other, but that didn't matter, I could already do quite a lot. I could go and lie at her side when she cried in bed, I could do the shopping. I told her what she should wear in the morning.

My father had been a man with a mustache who was away at sea for eight months in the year: so you'd say it didn't make all that difference whether she was married or divorced, but it made an awful lot of difference to her. My mother's a person who always knows the way everything ought to be done—after the divorce she'd become entirely unsure of herself. You could tell by little things. You could tell, for example, when the potatoes

for our evening meal were ready long before the greens or
the meat—and while I was sitting on a chair in the kitchen
just as in the past, watching her, full of admiration for her
timing, and to grind the nutmeg if need be, because I was
so fond of the shape of the little nutmeg grater, with its
rounded little tummy and its little box, complete with lid,
to catch the grains in—while I was sitting there I was struck
by the way she would often walk backwards and forwards,
unnecessarily, and even drop things. My capable mother. And
at night I'd hear the john flush four, five times: the worry had
given her diarrhea. The next morning she'd laugh about that
herself: I have to act so hard outwardly, she'd say, that I go
all soft inside as a reaction—and I'd laugh with her, but when
I heard the john flush three times in an hour, I didn't laugh
at all.

I saw to it that I went straight home after school in case
there was something I could do for her. I would make tea for
the two of us and we would drink it in the kitchen while
discussing how we'd tackle the problem of the evening meal.
I, who was so fond of departing from the rules, insisted we
have a hot meal every day—she ate so little, she was growing
so thin. And if my girl friends asked me to come and play at
their home I told them they'd have to come to mine. They
did, too, in the beginning, but I don't know, I couldn't really
show much interest in all that anymore, and after a while
they stayed away and I didn't miss them.

Four years passed in this way, years in which, it's true, I
did sit my entrance exam and passed, so changed schools and
had to deal with a separate teacher for each subject and a
class full of unfamiliar children—but what went on at school
only acquired significance when I told about it at home and
my mother said what she thought about it. My real life was

at home, where we did everything together, my mother and I, where I knew who I was, and where I was needed too, even though my mother now only rarely had any trouble with her stomach.

When I was fourteen my mother acquired a friend. I say a friend, but I mean Gerrit. He fell in love with her and she probably with him, although she didn't tell me as much, but that's how it must have been, for after a period during which she let me share her feelings less and less and I grew more and more unhappy because she was drawing away from me, there came a day when she said he was coming to live with us.

Just like that.

I hated him, and I hated her too for bringing him into our house. I hated the bedroom, I hated the sound of the john at night telling me how unneeded I had become. I hated the meals when everything I told about school would be heard by him too.

I began to come home less. I stopped drinking tea in the kitchen. I began to keep my mouth shut at table. And if my mother sought my company and wanted to talk to me I was purposely as rude as I could be, I said things to her that I knew would hurt her (I said she was getting old, I said she looked so awful I was ashamed of her). And then I hated myself. But hated her too, her too, because I knew she would go and talk to him about what she was sure to call my "problems with adapting." I hated her because she had betrayed me. I hated her because she was no longer mine.

Yes, I was jealous, but it took me a few months to realize it. For a long time I thought that she alone was responsible for the estrangement between us. Her feelings for me must have changed. She was behaving differently, wasn't she? I don't know, the atmosphere at home was exactly like that in a television ad—all forced cheerfulness, with mommie, poppie and teenage daughter. For instance, my mother began calling me "my darling" too, a thing she had never done before.

I began to feel sorry for myself. I drew in bags under my eyes with a lead pencil to appear pitiable, and hoped there'd be someone who'd notice how bad I looked, so they'd pay attention to me . . .

I was jealous but didn't recognize my feelings. After all, I had never before felt I wanted her to belong to me: you don't feel things that are natural as anything extraordinary.

It was a few months before I understood what I felt, and I was ashamed. Hating him didn't matter, but her—I didn't want that.

A teacher at my school once told me I am the sort of person who is good at coming to decisions. I decided to get used to the situation, because I did realize I could only master my feelings if I learned to accept his presence in the house. So I tried to. It wasn't easy and at night I'd cry in my bed because it was so difficult. But once I've started off on a thing, I go through with it, and I reminded myself why I was doing it. That helped. I didn't, after all, want to lose her love! And she could only love me if I liked him. So . . .

And so it came about that I didn't go upstairs that evening. My mother had a meeting, he and I were alone together in the house, and I stayed downstairs instead of going up and doing my homework, for I wanted there to be some contact between us.

I sat on the sofa, and he on one of the two chairs opposite. I was reading a pop magazine, he the *Weekly Post*. Minutes went by, then I slapped my magazine to and looked at him. Till he felt me looking at him.

"What are you reading about?" I asked.

"Oh," he said and laughed (actually it was that grown-ups' laugh I'd always disliked so much), "that wouldn't interest you."

"If it didn't interest me I wouldn't ask." I wasn't entirely honest—I wasn't really interested in what he was reading, but I did want to hear what he thought was interesting and how he'd talk about it.

As he was speaking (it was about trade unions and some agreement or other the Cabinet had come to with them and which some members of the government no longer wanted to keep to, something of that sort), I watched him and saw what attracted my mother in him. When he grew enthusiastic he had something attractive about him—I hadn't noticed it before, because he'd never been enthusiastic in my presence. So I tried to keep him talking by asking him questions (the difference between the two houses of Parliament, I'm always forgetting that), but there came a moment all the same when we had nothing left to talk about. So I just sat and smiled at him.

"Do you already have boy friends?" he then asked.

"At times," I said.

He looked at me for a moment, then stood up. "You'd like a drink, I bet," he said. "What shall I pour you?"

I didn't know. I never touch strong drink.

"I'm having a whisky," he said. "Care to join me?"

"All right," I said, and we drank whisky. I didn't enjoy the first glass, but he said you had to get used to the taste, so I took courage and went on drinking and, indeed, the second glass didn't taste so bad.

For a while we talked of other things, my school, his work (he does something in computers), and then he returned to the subject of my boy friends.

"What do you get up to with them?" he asked. He was really attractive when he smiled.

"Nothing special, a French kiss or two," I said, though it was none of his business.

He poured me out a third glass of whisky. "Aren't you curious to know what happens after that?" he asked. I looked at his hand which was clasping the bottle and was reminded of those advertisements in magazines in which men are holding bottles, and I saw his hand and I thought that's a man's hand, man's hand, and he bent over toward me after he'd put the bottle aside and he put his fingers under my chin so that I was forced to look at him and he smelled of tobacco, and he asked me again if I wasn't curious and suddenly I *was*, although I'd never been before, so I nodded.

And then we went to bed.

Since he'd been living with us my mother made breakfast in the mornings, and the next morning I was scared to go downstairs. I hung around as long as I could so that I'd have to rush through breakfast to get to school on time. But all she asked was if I'd slept well. Nothing else was said.

That afternoon I stayed away till dinnertime and when I got home he was already there. We sat down to table. Nothing unusual. And there was no tension either, everything was the same as at other times. Even he acted toward me exactly as before. As if nothing had happened, as though that thing between us had never taken place.

I went upstairs immediately after the meal, I was all confused. I didn't understand a thing about it. My mother is the sort of person who always reacts if anything happens, so she couldn't know. He hadn't told her. The rotter. My mother still didn't know a thing!

I thought about it that night in bed. I couldn't sleep. It kept going through my head, the way it was: he hadn't said anything, she didn't know about it, what would happen now, how would it go on from here?

There was only one solution, of course. I had to tell. I couldn't very well let myself be maneuvered into a situation where he and I would know something she didn't; I had no wish to share a secret with him. What we already shared was bad enough.

So, home from school the following day, I told her. I didn't say much, I simply told her what had happened.

She hardly believed it at first, then she grew very quiet, tense, I don't know, it was terrible the way she looked, it hurt to see her face, but she did look at me. All she asked was whether he had used a preventative and I said, yes, a condom, and she said, "Thank God," but she didn't, of course, sound at all grateful, "and now you go and do your homework."

Later I heard the awful sounds of quarreling downstairs, I couldn't help but cry about it, it reminded me of the days when my father was still living with us and, that made me afraid, for now everything would change just as it had then.

I knew it, and this time it was my fault.

It did change: he packed his bags and left.

But after he'd gone, things weren't the same as they'd been before. My mother and I went on acting coolly to each other. She no longer talked with me. He'd left, but he was more present in her thoughts than I was. She didn't see me. We shared our meals, she even went on getting the breakfast, but she didn't speak. Except to ask how was school today. Nothing more. And she didn't mention that evening again and never uttered Gerrit's name.

I understood what she meant. It was my fault he'd left,

that's why she was no longer speaking. That *I* was still there
had to be a punishment for her. She had had to choose between him and me and because I was still too young to look
after myself, she'd had to choose me, and now she hated me
because I had come between him and her and it was my fault
he'd left.

So the other thing had to be my fault too. That drinking, I
mean, and the sex with him.

Formerly, this was precisely what I would have liked to
talk to her about, because it was this that I was always thinking about. About how it had all been—dizzy-making, and
he'd made me curious, afterward it felt as though he'd
tricked me into it, but she was punishing me, so it really was
my fault.

Why did I do it? To revenge myself on her for having
brought him into the house? Because I'd be closer to her if I
went to bed with her lover? Am I crazy? Or sick?

After a week I was wishing she had sent *me* packing. I
couldn't concentrate any longer at school, and being at home
was even worse. But I didn't know how I could change it, I
didn't know what I ought to do.

Until one day, during the meal, someone rang her up. It
was so simple, yet it shocked me. It altered something. "Yes,"
she said into the receiver. "Lisbeth here." I'd heard her say it
hundreds of times before. Her name. Her first name. "Lisbeth." I've known my mother's name was Lisbeth since I was
a toddler. When I was little I even called her by that name
for a while. Lisbeth.

But that evening all at once it was something very important, the way she said her name, so naturally over the telephone, as though to her it was completely a matter of course
that she was called Lisbeth.

To me she was my mother, but to herself she was an individual. She was Lisbeth, a woman who had been divorced and had a daughter and who had had a lover. An individual who had lived for thirty-five years, twenty of them without me.

I couldn't sleep again that night, but more because I was excited rather than unhappy. And I understood what I had to do. I had to talk to her—to Lisbeth—even if I had to begin myself, because it was important to me to know what she thought of me and what she felt about that awful sex episode. And if she condemned me, if she condemned me, I had to know that too, for then, perhaps, she'd be able to show me why it was I'd done that with him and then I'd be able to change until I'd become someone she could respect again.

For I can't do without her. Not because she is my mother, but because of who she is.

I spoke her name. After school it was, I'd sat down at her side, I'd made tea just as in the old days, I poured her out a cup and gave it to her and spoke her name. She looked at me.

"I want to talk to you," I said. I was near to tears. "I want to know exactly what it is you are so angry with me about," I said. "Are you so sorry it's finished between you?"

She looked up then, at that question, then she looked at me *and she began to laugh.* And that took me by surprise again, it gave me such a shock that I suddenly began to cry very loudly, and then, and then she put her arms tightly around me and she said all sorts of things, poor child, she said, how could I know you were blaming yourself, no, of course I'm not sorry, she said, that blackguard, such a rotter to take advantage of your curiosity, no, she said, it isn't that, I am sorry, it's true, I'm sorry because something that could have been very special for you and that you could have found out about all on your own in your own time, that he should have robbed you of that, that's what I'm sorry about, she said, my baby, I didn't say anything because you said nothing, I thought let's forget this unpleasant episode as soon as possible, as soon as possible.

So now everything is just as it was before he came. Just as before. But I don't know whether I'm happy about it.

BLITZ-FORTUNE

Muriel Cerf   MANUEL BIDERMANAS

MURIEL CERF *was born in Paris, June 4, 1950.*

After passing her Baccalauréat she studied at the École du Louvre, where she specialized in the art of China, India, and Japan. At the same time she studied drawing at a small school in the rue de la Pompe.

Later she attended the École Nationale des Langues Orientales, first in the Persian, then in the Chinese department.

After the death of a friend caused by a right-wing organization during the 1968 student unrest, she became disillusioned with the university, but gained a diploma at the École du Louvre.

In the meantime she traveled in Asia, Africa, America, the Indian Ocean, and Polynesia.

Muriel Cerf has been writing since her childhood. On her return from the Indies in 1970, she edited her travel notes and determined to live entirely by her writing.

She went back to Asia and spent a year in India and Indonesia. Then returned to Paris and worked for brief periods, first for Le Figaro *and then for* L'Express.

She wrote L'Antivoyage *and sent it to Gallimard, where it was accepted by Roger Caillois, Claude Roy, Claude Gallimard and André Malraux. As Gallimard could not undertake to bring the book out in less than six months, however, and she needed money, she accepted the offer of immediate publication made by Simone Gallimard of Mercure de France.*

Her next five books appeared under the same imprint. Une Passion *was her first book to be published by Jean-Claude Lattès.*

Forthcoming books: A play; "a very cheerful book about the suicide of a thirty-year-old girl in Venice"; and three volumes on Mexico.

BLITZ-FORTUNE
by Muriel Cerf

TRANSLATED FROM THE FRENCH
BY BARBARA WRIGHT

That evening, in the restaurant of the Hôtel de Paris, she had sent back all the main courses and, for dessert, had just eaten a few mouthfuls of an imponderable soufflé au Grand Marnier, while he was unashamedly giving himself a chocolate fix. A veritable exploit, to put away such an enormous portion of that Christian-choking gâteau called Charlotte, but since he was a Jew it was probably easier for him to get it down. She was rather rudely drumming on the table, her eyes lowered to conceal her boredom and disgust from her young fiancé—she loved him, though—the future luminary of the bar whom she was to marry in Paris in three weeks' time, with a reception at the Pré Catelan and all that jazz. And the young Counselor, Maître Charles-Henri Shurakian, was licking his chocolate-covered chops, quite oblivious of the melancholy mood of his fiancée sitting opposite him, drinking her coffee and staring into the black beverage as if she was reading a future of a similar color in it, and also rereading an equally schwarz event in the very recent past. Viz: the half hour before they left the hotel, those thirty minutes which had sufficed for the fiancé to screw her clumsily and lick off

her sober but judicious makeup with his canine tongue. In
the café, then, she repudiated him for the first time, because
of an inadequate, totally ineffectual fuck, and a greed which
showed signs of a suppressed desire which, *sotto voce*, she described as bulimia. Not without reason.

"Why don't we go to the Casino?" she murmured, to alle-
viate her boredom.

"To Loews?" he suggested prudently, hoping desperately
that she'd be content to amuse herself with slot machines.

"No. I said to the Casino."

Whoever says casino says roulette, and she had on her
hijacker's expression, which made him shudder. He remembered the pathetic fuck, told himself that the girl wanted to
be jumped in quite a different way, he was moved to pity,
called himself a triple nonentity, she had felt a surge of
adrenalin—so rare in a pure intellectual—and he hadn't
satisfied her . . . Poor darling. Let her go and have her fling
at the Casino, then. She adored gambling. A problem for the
future. And only roulette, risk and vertigo, she never cooked
up any sort of martingale, never read anything on gaming
theory, just played according to the clairvoyance of witches
and sometimes got away with it, to the amazement of the
croupiers. "My wife is a witch," René Clair film. He'd have
to make the best of it—he was going to marry a girl who
didn't have a bean but who on the other hand made use of
paranormal powers. He wouldn't let her gamble away the
meager royalties she received from the publication of her
poems and the performances of her plays in the provinces. It
had to be admitted: his little fiancée was excessively broke.
He would let her squander the inheritance he hoped to be receiving shortly from his father—also an attorney, and prema-
turely doddery. But that evening the young fellow felt obscurely menaced, bamboozled, for there was far too much
determination in the expression of the game-loving creature
facing him, but what if the said creature was quite simply in-
tending to gamble with her destiny, what if it was none other
than THEIR destiny that was at stake that night, and what if

this stake implicated him to a degree he couldn't even think of without terror, for this girl's destiny—don't be ashamed to imagine it!—he had vehemently decided to link with his own. No, he was getting ideas into his head. She was merely going to chuck a thousand francs down the drain and give herself a kick at the Casino. He'd be keeping a close watch on her!

And, in any case, there was good reason for keeping her under close surveillance. Beautiful, his fiancée. Thirty years old, but looked twenty. Her entry into restaurants and casinos always created a stir, and not, alas, among the indigent, but among the emirs, who would clearly like to take her by assault with the same impetuosity with which they tried to break the bank of Monte Carlo. Total failure with the bank, and as for Mademoiselle Esther Lydie Laméra, his fiancée, he guffawed, not the slightest chance, THE CLOSEST SURVEILLANCE. That evening, draped in a single eau-de-Nil gauze veil, as transparent as a gauze bandage, attached by two ruched straps to shoulders of flinty and refined thinness, she displayed the extreme crystalline beauty that precedes an attack of nerves, a divorce, or momentous decisions. Her bony kneecaps made her magnificent rag dress flutter, and she was as naked underneath it as an Iranian woman in her chador after bathing at Babolsar in the days when they were allowed to make merry on the shores of the Caspian, always providing they didn't get themselves killed in a car crash on the way there—a frequent occurrence. He disapproved of her nudity under her rags, but, thinking of Babolsar, felt an uprush of fascination for his fiancée, one of the only women to have penetrated into the holy city of Qum in the days of the Pahlavis, at the risk of being lynched . . . From her eighteenth year on, this wild girl had held sway over the four continents. He was determined that once she was married she would discover a fifth—the Shurakian continent—and forget the others. An arduous task. But he was prepared to accept it. He loved her, for goodness' sake, he loved his exceptional, crazy, playwriting poetess, soon to be his wife, his wife in three weeks' time. And he had recently found her morose, mutilated, indulgent, indifferent, different from the enthusiastic, capricious, impassioned, crazy girl that he used to know. Yes, kind of maimed. Ever since they had been at Monte Carlo she had smoked two packs of Virginia cigarettes a day, drunk too much, eaten nothing, and, when he screwed her, had stared fixedly at the ceiling, all the while appearing to lend an absentminded ear to the amorous sibilants issuing from her fiancé. (In actual fact, at these precious moments she was listening to the soapy sound of the sea hitting the rocks at the foot of the Old Beach Hotel, she was listening with pleasure to that long, silky slap, which then turned into a kind of confused crackle, and was so close . . .) In short, she wasn't interested in what she was doing, and, her betrothed concluded, this was all wrong. He was worried, obviously. Knowing that he wasn't crazy enough for her. He, a man of the law; she, a woman who transgressed all laws. Diurnal and nocturnal. He, Jovian; she, Saturnian. Jews, both of them; Sephardim, both of them, but she was a Zionist, and he hated everything to do with Israel, with rabbinical folklore, and with the sabra generation. He considered that this Salome would always need to seduce the whole world, to charm everything down to the very handles of the prison doors, always supposing that some lucky fellow managed to incarcerate her, and that even when she had got the prison guard under her spell she would still need her Monte Carlo shows, her fireworks, her *feste del Redentore* in Venice, the eternal spring of Cuernavaca, in Mexico, where she went to write her yearly play in the house of one of her friends, those innumerable, mysterious and appalling friends—he couldn't slay them all, especially the faraway ones. He considered that she would always need miracles, and he wasn't the man to produce them, and anyway he didn't believe in them; that she would need to spend a month every year at the Hotel Danieli in Venice (a month entirely devoted to writing poetry); that she would always need *Impromptus de Versailles*, and he was far too hardworking to create them—God, how exhausting this girl was, but that was precisely why he was crazy about her, why he forced himself to hump her in telephone booths with transparent glass sides because she had assured him that this was the very greatest chic, and in fact she adored being taken by surprise on all fronts, as for example diamonds, well, he had to give them to her when she was least expecting them, otherwise both the pleasure and the luster of the bluish-white stones were diminished. In short, he not only had to blow his father's fortune on her, he also had to exhaust the treasure-house of his imagination . . . And finally, she needed to be near her indispensable girl friends—was she a lesbian?—and female confidantes, whom she probably liked far more than she let him know. As they went into the Casino he was feeling somewhat discouraged.

Basically, there were probably only two things that excited her sexually: gambling with her own life, and having multifarious passions for multifarious people, countries, animals, or even flowers. He had already managed to distance her from the people; she had given them up in favor of the tête-à-tête. *Dialoghi d'amore.* Well, yes—perhaps. She was bored. He was undermining himself. He promised her countries—with him; animals—in common; flowers—in a window box in their future apartment. She gave him a pathetic little smile. And what if she said no at the sacramental moment? A thirty-year-old vagabond, marrying for the first time, is quite capable of making a U-turn, especially this one, born a Scorpio, with Pluto in Leo, and Pluto in Leo was a veritable disaster. Esther: blood, fire and air, elusive, mercurial water, white spirit, gun cotton—nothing you could get your hands on, nothing but a burning evanescence, and this was precisely what made her seem more beautiful to him, precisely what had given him the *idée fixe* of taming this firebrand, of extinguishing her, even, of ringing this migratory bird. This had soon been done, and there was a strange expression in her eyes when she looked at the glittering ring on her third finger . . . In his defense, it must be said that Maître Charles-Henri was madly in love with his crackpot, the only condition approaching madness he had ever experienced. A pathetic, mute kind of madness that no longer dazzled the gambler, who was now avid for other thrills, and making her way, cleaving her way through the crowd, like an eau-de-Nil-rigged sailing vessel, toward one of the roulette tables.

"No—I have some dough."

And now she was refusing to gamble away her future husband's money. Feeling castrated, he chewed the gall of wrath, which tasted of dandelions. She took some bills out of her bag and exchanged them for jetons—about a thousand francs, he estimated, spying on her. She turned around, saw him standing there behind her, and phosphoresced with rage. Always watching her. What if she did want to chuck ten thousand down the drain, that was her business, wasn't it? Actually, she was broke. So it was only one thousand, because she couldn't live on what she earned from her playwriting. *You don't need to worry anymore, my darling—I'm here.* Every time she heard this refrain she gritted her teeth, felt her bones quiver, and her smooth, oriental Jewess's skin go lumpy.

"Do me a favor—go for a walk. I'll leave at midnight, whether I've won or lost. But don't stay stuck there behind me, it brings me bad luck. Please, darling."

He obeyed. He'd go and wander around the square, avoiding the Rolls-Royces, and praying that no Arab petrol sheikh would spot her and slip her some jetons. Naked under her absorbent gauze, the bitch. And he, a Spanish Jew; he, hideously jealous; he, the Moor with his crazy Ophelia, no, his innocent Desdemona. Jealous, and embroiled in melodramatic pathos; and she, perversely beautiful under the shower of the Casino's diamantine lights; she, a prey to her own vertigo, with a tiny trace of sweat between her breasts, and God knew that that dress (well, that thing, that tunic: if only it would burn her, as Nessus's garment burned the tender flesh of Deianira!) God knew that that dress was décolletée.

Someone would notice that trace of sweat, that delicate dew, where there was the sparkle of the blue sequins she habitually scattered over her solar plexus. The she-devil had sublime breasts, out of proportion to her equivocal thinness; heavy breasts whose areolae were so like a handful of blackberries . . . Shut up, you jealous fool, leave her be, her and her breasts, let her tempt fortune with her royalties, just be a stupid feminist, let her live, don't impose yourself on her. Love makes you clumsy, spineless, sluggish, deformed; it makes you prognathic, because you're always pointing a suspicious chin; it gives you conjunctivitis, because you've become a dirty voyeur, so you're always tiring your eyes; and that was certainly the way she saw him, as ugly as an Indian vulture devouring its meager carcass. That must be the way she saw him because she was frigid, because she wouldn't let him grab hold of her bony knees with his big, masculine hands, as if they were a bird of prey's claws cruelly digging into her patella, because when he threw her down onto a bed she looked up at the ceiling with huge, bored eyes, sometimes darkened with a kind of rage, and he didn't dare meet this quasi-dead look from beyond the tomb, drifting toward an elsewhere in which he would never meet her . . . A place which is not of this world, and, as he well knew, is very far removed from the topic defined by the doctors under the name of orgasm, a word that made her turn pale, because she considered it abject. He also knew very well that this thirty-year-old girl had been something of a female Casanova, in order to have some basis on which to compare the men who came between her and God's stars, who lay on top of her and refused to let her observe the astral bodies, which she was passionately interested in. So she was in a position to make comparisons, and he had never gone about it so badly with any other girl. Too crazy about her. Lost control, hence premature end to the operations: he was familiar with the slight contraction of disgust of Esther's lips after the assault, the ironic commiseration with which she contemplated the blotch of sperm ejac-

ulated onto her hollow stomach, and then the lively fervor
with which she wiped it away with a Kleenex, and then the
moment when her mouth, with its thick, mango-like texture,
gradually relaxed into the mocking smile of someone who is
delighted that the chore has taken so little time.

"My love, do you still want to marry me?"

This had been at the time of the reprehensible chocolate
Charlotte, on the terrace of the Hôtel de Paris; the night was
gradually turning the roofs of the Casino blue, and metamor-
phosing them into Moorish, onion-shaped domes; the per-
fumes of Araby were floating in the air. Esther had turned to
look at him—the whites of her eyes were even more dazzling
in the darkness—then she had looked down at the portion of
Charlotte with the same resigned commiseration as when he
had eja . . .

Esther, lost in thought, as fragile as the wafer she was carefully breaking into little pieces with veiled wrath—God knew
what she was transferring onto that wafer!—had said sweetly:

"Have I ever suggested that I had changed my mind,
Charles-Henri? I am ringed, my bird-catcher. For as long as
you see this malefic band of sapphires and diamonds impris-
oning my third finger, my dear man, you'll have nothing to
worry about. And anyway, I prefer not to know why you
stuff yourself with chocolate gâteaux as if they were Valium.
If you become a potbelly, I'll repudiate you. Become a zombie if you must, that wouldn't worry me. (Meaning: you'd
worry me less.) Therefore, I am ringed. Confine yourself to
appearances. (Meaning: you haven't got what it takes to
rebel against them.)"

Ringed. She had hurled this word at him like a challenge, a
glove that he hadn't picked up, with the bitterness of the
doomed, who seem to be offering up their sorrows to God.
He had said nothing. This had been an hour before, so it was
already in the past. He couldn't stand it any longer. Something was happening in the Casino in his absence. Guys were
picking her up. Before she went into the gaming room she

had made herself up with a coat of lipstick that was even thicker than lacquer, so that way, what with the slash in the middle, it was impossible for anyone not to notice her feline face, and cats were a race he had always distrusted, preferring dogs, those eternal beggars for love, those reservoirs of gratitude. He climbed up the steps to the Casino, determined to track her down, but to remain hidden. Though in any case, hypnotized as she was by that accursed roulette table, he could have crushed three of her toes and stubbed his cigarette out on her shoulder without her even noticing. *Avanti*, he told himself, pathetic and courageous.

Esther had very few jetons left. He estimated that there were two hundred francs in the little pile in front of her. She had lost the rest, and this gave him abominable pleasure. But she looked rather more as if she was hatching up some act of clairvoyance than suffering a defeat. He saw her push her modest pile *en plein* onto number twenty-six. Right, she was going to lose the lot, and then say there was a jinx on her.

"Twenty-six, black, *pair* and *passe*."

A number that pays thirty-five for one. Jesus Christ, he swore.

A deep breath lifted up the famous breasts, the greeny-brown eyes sparkled, and she replaced her winnings on the twenty-six. Absolutely nuts, he told himself. I'm going to marry a nut. What's more, she lives the way she gambles. *Les jeux sont faits, rien ne va plus*. There she is with her twenty-six in her head, and *rien ne . . .*

"Twenty-six, black, *pair* and *passe*."

Excitement all around the table. The old lady, who was always given fifty francs to play with and whom the croupier had to nudge awake every so often when she completely collapsed over the table, stopped snoring and put a chip on the twenty-six. Esther exchanged a strange smile with this old lady, and hesitated for a second. Charles-Henri saw her on the point of putting it all back on that magic number,

three times oh no she was going to bollix it up avoid that she
really is acting like a dope besides it's midnight MIDNIGHT
VICTORY stop her playing—she was going to lose two hundred and fifty thousand. And then he couldn't control himself any longer, everything happened very rapidly, he rushed
up behind her, grabbed her wrist, pushed her stake onto the
twenty-nine, in the unconscious fear that she was going to
win once again, and that just because she was a medium she
would be putting twenty-five million old francs in her
pockets and never need him anymore, and that this win
meant—he obscurely felt—the symbolic rupture of their en-
gagement and Esther's return to her autonomy. She stiffened,
her face became frozen as if under a crust of snow, though he
could only see it in profile; one of her shoulders suddenly
dropped as if under the hand of grim Fate, like the time
when a saleswoman in the Galeries Lafayette had caught her
red-handed in the act of shoplifting, which had happened to
her in her salad days. Copped by reality. Nabbed. Licked,
she watched the wheel rolling as she stood up, her dress like a
flag of hope at half-mast, her lips pallid under the savage lipstick the color of ripe cherries, her cheeks livid beneath the
slash of purple makeup underlining the high, almost Asiatic,
cheekbones.

"Twenty-six, black, *pair* and *passe*."

The old lady, after an apologetic glance at the ramrod-stiff
young woman, a statue of defeat, a Tarot card, no thicker,
threw herself onto the jetons she owed to the girl in green.
The girl in green smiled at the old lady, shrugged her shoulders, left the table, and the voyeurs scattered to make way
for this creature whose forehead had become almost taurine,
and whose distended eyes were sharpening themselves like
two threatening javelins, when the possessor of these marvels
—forehead and eyes, among other things—bumped into a hag-
gard young man who tried to hold her back but she carried
on regardless, trod on his toes, and went out in a flurry of
green gauze, and the young woman disappeared, and hope
disappeared with her.

She was walking in the direction of the Old Beach Hotel, she shivered, she'd left without her shawl, but the said shawl landed on her shoulders, placed there by the falsely benevolent hands of the young man who heard her muttering: twenty-six, twenty-six, twenty-six . . . Nine, the inversion of the number, inversion is a satanic sign . . .

She turned around and faced the enemy and official fiancé.

"Get lost. Scram. Never again. How could you dare. I was going to win two hundred and fifty thousand. I was going to escape you, no doubt. So young, and he's already buying a wife. How many camels, in your opinion, to buy me? Filthy pro-Arab. Anti-Jewish Jew. Renegade. Hand of Belial. Maniac. Shamefaced Yid. Premature ejaculator. Whistler in bathrooms after act manqué. The only suitors I love passionately are my publishers, who suggest, checkbook in hand, that I should write novels and give up the *succès d'estime* stuff— poems and plays, that is. I'm going to write for my living. Thrillers. Science fiction. Well-documented history, you'll see. I'm giving up being Rimbaud and Shakespeare, just for you to leave me in peace. Beat it with your filthy dough. Be-ee-eat it. Drop dead. Drop dead, and take the bastards who wish you well with you. How could I have? Ah yes, your handsome mug, typical of the Jews from Oran, you oriental wog hoodlum. Your dialectical gifts . . . ruined by too much study, my dear boy. Law and political sciences, plus the homosexual love of a Marxist prof, people don't get over that. But on the other hand, they lead to a career. The supreme career of an attorney, right there waiting for you, you only have to stoop. To stoop, because personally I don't put the men of the bar very high. Okay, you love me madly, but apart from that, you know what you do for me?—you jinx me. Love doesn't exist. There isn't any area in the brain allotted to love, you know. But jinxes exist. No one knows which part of the brain they belong to, but there's proof positive of the existence of the phenomenon. Perverse, abject masochist, you can't move, you've turned into a pillar of salt. So you like it, when I insult you? My fiancé! Oh, that was too much,

wasn't it, a quarter of a million in my pocket, no more obli-
gations toward anybody for a short while, just as, if I pro-
duced a best-seller, that would also be too much, what you
want is for me to be kept on the library's reserve shelves until
the time comes for me to be used in school textbooks. You
want teachers to give dictation from the works of Laméra.
But the last thing you want is for her to be covered with
laurels in her lifetime or in mine, otherwise (and I'm speaking
with your mouth—that sewer)—otherwise, I would have to
become at least the President of the Bar, and if I didn't make
it, that would be real castration. Antediluvian creature. Go
and marry an Iranian woman in a chador. Well, you can't do
that anymore. Go back to the Maghreb."

Daughter of Scorpio, twin sister of the "red" star Antares,
lousy bitch, he thought, here you are, in three minutes,
demolishing a destiny, OUR destiny, that "our" which made
you turn pale even when I used it for the first time, with
such delight. And me—I'm condemned once again. The first
time, I was only twelve years old, and it was by the secret
fascist army, the OAS, for harboring an Arab.

"Ah, your famous exploit, before they rushed you off
quick to the big city! The black-bordered letter your mother
received, telling her that the OAS were out to get her son, or
something like that!" (The witch, she really could read your
thoughts.) "I only have to see your hangdog look to know
what you're thinking of . . ."

He hung his head. Walking very quickly, they had got to
Loews. She stopped short. Studied him with irritation, and a
great deal of fatalism. "*Alea jacta est*," she said. "The whole
thing was contained in that symbol of the inverted number.
You've been bringing me bad luck for a whole year now, my
poor friend. And for a whole year you've been bugging me
with your jealousy. And screwing me so lousily. And boring
me. And refusing to understand, you great egoist, that if I am
the *Theatrum Mundi* (your own words) for you, for me
you're nothing but a poor puppet now, and I'm already too

old for puppets. I used to agree with Montherlant about marriage. I almost changed my mind. What happened? It was the monumental gaffe you made just now. There's absolutely no way you can make up for it. It's all quite clear now. I shall never marry anyone. And in any case, I should make you unhappy. I should be unfaithful to you with other men, with girls, with the sun and the sea, I should be unfaithful to you when I was biting into a sour apple, and I should never be more unfaithful to you than when I was writing, because there's no way in which you could be present in my writing. We're poison to each other. You need me, you say. Go and tell that to your mother. She'll be in the seventh heaven to hear such talk from her beloved son. You should thank God that you have an Algerian-born French mother, and that you're an only son. Me, I'm neither your mother, nor Algerian-born, nor in the marriage stakes. I'm a hermaphrodite, a spinster, a vagabond, a writer without a bean. Fate willed you to push my hand onto the twenty-nine, and I was taken by surprise and didn't resist. Thank you, Fate. That's what's called coming to the assistance of a person in danger. You were more in danger than I was. After a year of matrimony we'd both have been sent to the loony bin. Now, for the last time, you're going to be leonine—proud and generous. Obey your sign of the zodiac. Give the daughter of Scorpio, that lousy bitch, a few pesos—*I* know what you're cooking up in the region of your brain-box—so she can go and play games with the slot machines. After that I'll go back to the Old Beach Hotel, pack my bags, and be in Paris tomorrow, and then I'll go around the world again. Yep. A decision made just as rapidly as your gesture. Monte Carlo, the town of eccentricity, where the rivers change beds. Me too. To get back to my own. Alone. I'm not leaving you for another ape. I'm leaving you for myself, which in some cases is saying no little, but which is saying nothing at all at the times when I'm disgusted with myself. At this moment, for instance, because I'm hurting you."

She added, to herself: Poor child! "The outstretched arms

of need; the upstretched arms of desire"—yes, Monsieur Barthes. I can't stand that need any longer, nor the security he offers me. The more security he gives me, the more tranquilizers I have to take. In my vocabulary, security equals claustrophobia. Marriage is impossible. Poor child. I love you, he says, with biblical simplicity. I am not simple, and neither is the Bible, I can never see why people bracket those two words. I shall never marry anyone—except the universe. Poor child.

He fumbled in his pockets, brought out a hundred-franc bill, and gave it to her. It was as if he was the one receiving alms, and she the Lady Bountiful. She burst out laughing, and he hated her.

Pathetic, cheap sentiment. Love. An occidental myth. If you were in class, Shurakian, your teacher would tell you that you could do better. Find out why you have an obsessional need to fuck and fuck and fuck, even when your partner makes such a botch of it, why you always need a presence by your side, oh so heartwarming, to justify your existence, why you insist on being wed, on signing a bit of paper that incarcerates you with someone who hasn't done any harm, why you're so scared of solitude, why you have to eat compensatory chocolate gâteaux, why the world doesn't gratify you unless you have a bored girl with you, why your colossal shortage of love, why the obligatory shithouse of sex, tongue stuff and billing and cooing, why that convict prison so highly thought of by other people, why want to drag me into that twofold nightmare, when you know very well that I shall never stop writing, fourteen hours a day if I feel like it, and that I shall therefore never have slightest need of exercises in bed, or chocolate, or holidays, or the cinema, or of any of the palliatives offered (or rather, sold for a lot of money) to all the mentally deficient—you included—who will never explain anything, and who'll go on clobbering me with the magic words *I love you*. My mother used to say them to my father too, and in the end he committed suicide. Out of boredom, and a lot of other things. Thanks for the hundred francs. I'm an old woman, Charles-Henri, I'm thirty years old, and I'm certainly passing up my last chance not to end my days alone. All I can tell you is—it gives me a kick. *Shalom aleichem.*

She went into Loews. Rushed off to the WC and spewed out her soul—she'd never been so cruel, but she'd had to do it; poor kid, he'd have come and held her head if he'd known. He must be hanging around outside Loews, waiting for her. Like glue. The mythical glue of the sentimental lover. Nauseated, she threw up for the last time, then washed her face, renewed her makeup, and went out of the WC feeling horribly guilty; this breakup was an absolute crime, but something had to save her from that marriage, which would have been slow murder. She felt cold. Chilled to the marrow, she went over to the slot machines. Ah yes, get change for the bill, what was she thinking of? Alas, she was still imagining her head on her fiancé's shoulder, her nose in his black, cherubic curls, breathing the vanilla-scented aroma of the back of his neck. To hell with reminiscences. She changed her bill and began playing like a Fury, looking neither to right nor to left, utterly unhappy, if he committed suicide she would be responsible, oh no oh no, let him go and pick up a floozy in Régine's and screw her rather than playing Werther. Though that was his style. His eyes full of fatal romances. Forget him. Wipe him off the map. Coins came tumbling down, she had bewitched the flashing machine. She got on well with this machine, she talked to it, confided to it what had just happened to her and how she was going to return to her monastic life, go back to her beloved studies and never again tolerate a man in her vicinity, whereupon her accomplice, the machine, delighted, disgorged whole piles of money. When the receptacle was full to overflowing she gathered up the coins and, as she was stuffing them into her bag—the evening bag that he had given her—she was on the point of weakening, of running after him and apologizing, and—a certainty—of ruining her life, so as not to have to take the blame. Oh misery, she thought, I've been had, I . . .

"Bullshit! Damn it! *Madre mia de Guadalupe!* This shitty machine . . ."

She turned toward her left, where the curses were coming from. Witches always come from the left. She was a witch, no doubt about that, the half-caste (Cuban? Puerto Rican? Mexican?—some Indian blood in her, in any case), as desirable as an unkept promise, this androgynous *novillera* was a witch. (Esther saw herself, ten years previously, in this girl, her eternally pursued, sought-after double, her marvelous reflection—saw herself impatiently kicking a slot machine with the same vigorous action of the calf, the same movement of the heel, and if this novillera, given her appetency to destroy everything that resisted her, and, at a fair guess, to abandon anything that no longer resisted her, wasn't born with Scorpio in the ascendant, it was enough to make you doubt the decrees of the stars.) This witch, frowning with Mephisophelean eyebrows, was still punching the robot, while the Greek Ilynx, the bird of vertigo, was wheeling around in her eyes. Before she had got to the point, not of demolishing the machine, which was a tough native of Maryland or Chicago, but of damaging her feet, in spite of the resistance of the sneakers they were clad in, Esther ironically handed her a fistful of five-franc pieces.

Looks. Thunderbolts. Cerebral turmoil. A ballet started, the only witness of which was the inevitable Charles-Henri, for the inevitable hadn't been able to stop himself, after taking a couple of turns around the square, from going into Loews, there to seek his Eurydice, which latter was resolutely turning her back on the conjugal hell and had just discovered one of those girls who made you quite certain that the best thing about Adam was his rib, which God had unfortunately deprived him of.

The androgynous half-caste took the coins, introduced seven, one after the other, into the slot designed for that purpose, pulled the delightful lever, stared with glaucous eyes at the jerky rotation of the bells and citrus fruits on the bands, won, smiled in naïve stupefaction at the donor of the coins, the donor also began playing again, they played and won in the same rhythm, their eyes riveted together, hooked, fascinated, entranced, victorious over the "one-armed bandit," the oneiric Coin-operated Machine. The hidden prowler, Maître Charles-Henri, was watching, and providing himself with excellent reasons to hate Esther, and hence to suffer less in the future. The facts had to be faced: these two dusky girls were fornicating under his very eyes. His fiancée had never looked at *him* like that. The shameless bitches were casting a spell over each other, and also casting a spell over the robot, even though it was a tricky thing with its own insidious autonomy. The coins came showering out, they pulled down their levers simultaneously, desired each other, all beauty is in the face, the body doesn't exist, only the irreal is desirable, the real doesn't interest anyone—a gap in the sky, said Esther's eyes, you're ebony, you're jet-black, your eyes are like malachite, I've never seen pupils of a deeper green, only Satan's third eye . . . and the coins still came tinkling down into the receptacle, and the machine itself had become desire, and play, and gift, and challenge, and the machine, circumvented through having been given such sexual pleasure, was on the point of exploding, as was Maître Charles-Henri, except that he was really not experiencing any sexual pleasure. What was taking place was an offense against public morals, but he was the only person to know it.

It seemed to the watcher, a real prison warden, that the scene had lasted a century. In front of him the wantons were silently plighting their troth, the only sound being the robotic whirring and clinking, a kind of orgy, Charles-Henri told himself, they're fucking in a threesome, the two unblushing lesbians (thinking of the ugly side of this word, so convenient for describing feminine friendships, which are always, of course, somewhat "special") and their one-armed bandit, who was buying their sordid favors (a vulgar way of putting it, but how he wished to throw dirt on those brazen bitches!) . . .

The somber little girl from the Americas was resolutely, solemnly pulling the handle toward her as if she were pressing the trigger of a safari rifle designed to kill elephants, and Esther made the same movement (witches masturbating on their broomsticks, Maître Charles-Henri thought grimly), though with even more suppleness, overcome with pleasure, observing with jubilation the pink-varnished shells over the little girl's nails, the too vivid spots of rouge over her Aztec cheekbones. Spellbound, Esther pulled the lever down toward her again—more gently than the Aztec—the game lasted for about fifteen minutes, during which time Maître Charles-Henri, the Prison Guard, decided either to crash his car or, like losing gamblers (and that was exactly his situation—he'd lost her at the gambling table, she owed her liberty to the *Société des Bains de Mer*, which had made or broken many other destinies) to throw himself off the top of the cliff at le Rocher, designed for just such a purpose, or from the Ravin de Sainte Dévote . . .

One last metallic flood came tumbling into what Esther poetically called "the spittoon," she looked to see whether the same thing was happening in the adjoining spittoon, observed with delight that it was, grabbed up the money with her thin, rapacious hands and juggled with it, the half-caste did the same, they both gurgled with laughter, their eyes still harpooned together, the gleam of grace shimmering over their faces, then looked at each other with a smile that would remain engraved on their faces for life. To Maître Charles-Henri this laughter was a knell, and he felt himself cut to the quick by the two dazzling displays of teeth slashing the dim

light of the Casino. It's all over, he told himself, and all because of a six changed into a nine, and in the time it takes for
the diabolical bandit's one arm to be lowered and released.
They've had me, these midnight girls, you only have to look
at them, their eyes like piercing spears, then wide-open and
incredulous, they're like sliding doors, their eyes, the bas-
tardess on the left must come from the Bering Strait but she'll
have had an Indian father, with that complexion. Esther always liked wogs, which is how I got my chance, great,
there's still a bit of irony left in me, I've played the watchdog
long enough. I've lost. They've found each other. Esther is
capable of decamping with her melting-pot beauty this very
evening. A conjugal ghost, repudiated before the wedding, he
departed.

I want to write the truth. He didn't even try to commit suicide. He valued his life, everyone has his weaknesses. A kind
of inertia fell upon him like a leaden cloak. Two months
later, Charles-Henri married a little débutante from the
French aristocracy; she had colorless eyes, her family was
cleaned out, but it had the sort of noble name that every petit
bourgeois from Oran aspires to be associated with, even if he
can't flaunt it himself. He was tremendously bored. This one
wasn't a gambler, you understand.

Other events of bewildering strangeness occurred under
the aegis of the *Société des Bains de Mer*.

Monte Carlo—an impossible fête. A permanent vortex.
Esther followed the half-caste to Mexico, lived with her in
the San Angel district, became a Mexican resident, heard that
France was on the verge of collapse (1982), and thought that
if her fiancé's hand had not diverted the course of destiny she
would no doubt have been up shit creek and in France at the
moment when everything was caving in. Just as well, just as
well, she told herself, sunbathing on the Pacific coast with

Inès, the half-caste, vowing to be on her guard against people who turned signs upside down and, from then on, to offer herself only to the sun. Just as well, just as well—her first novel, translated into Spanish, brought her precisely twice as much as she had nearly won at the Casino. Seven hundred thousand francs, or one hundred and seventy thousand dollars. Nothing explicitly physical ever took place between Inès and Esther, the twenty-year-old Mexican and thirty-year-old Jewess. But much more. They never betrayed their midnight oath. Esther came to adore the country of her exile—she was a Jewess, hence from nowhere—she forgot the grayness of a France at half-mast, and thought of Inès as her sister—Inès, the chocolate-colored archangel who had shown the way to the child of a people who were even more migratory than the great birds of passage in the Mexican sky.

She wasn't sure what to do with the ring. Should she leave it as a votive offering on the chasuble of a saint in a church in Guerrero? Give it to an Aztec girl paddling in a canal in Xochimilco? Toss it into that same canal? She sold it to a jeweler, and gambled the dough on the Mexican lottery. She won just enough to buy herself a terracotta Tree of Life, complete with Adam, and Eve, and the serpent, and even with a leopard. She put this naïf candelabrum in the lobby of her apartment and endowed it with candles which were lit every evening. Thus contemplating, every evening, the flight of Adam and Eve, she blessed her solitary paradise and felt that she was in the deepest hollow of the loop of time, as infrangible and melodic as the orbs of the Plumed Serpent.

MAR

Montserrat Roig   PILAR AYMERICH

MONTSERRAT ROIG *was born in Barcelona in 1946. She writes in the Catalan language and was awarded two Catalan literary prizes. As soon as her books were translated into Castilian she became an overnight success throughout Spain. She is also an expert and lively interviewer. Her television program called* People *so infuriated the State-owned Catalan television that she was dismissed, in spite of the general protest this decision unleashed.*

MAR

by Montserrat Roig

TRANSLATED FROM THE SPANISH
BY HELEN R. LANE

To M. B.
"Life has taught me to think, but
thinking has not taught me to live."
HERZEN

Two years have gone by since you went away, Mar, leaving me so alone it's obscene, two years since that day when your Mehari went over a cliff in the Tossas Pass and they brought you to the hospital and stuck tubes everywhere in you, a brutal rape in the name of science, two years since that day I saw you through the germ-proof glass, your head shaved completely bare, and you looked at me without seeing me because you were very far away, so far away you couldn't poke fun at my feminist theories now and scream at me that children don't belong to anybody, two years that have stopped me dead in my tracks in a kind of permanent freeze-frame shot, two years that force me to conclude that the woman I was when I was with you was simply a lie you helped invent, an illusion, and that the sort of life you were leading couldn't help but end the way it did, with all those tubes stuck in you, breathing because that was what had been ordered by those men in white who didn't know anything about the two of us, and if they

had known they would merely have said the same thing everybody else did, that you and I were having an affair, because they don't have any other words to define what began
to happen between us, and I wouldn't have known what to
call it either, Mar, just imagine, even after devouring all those
countless books on feminism, even after all those years and
years at the university, not to mention the taste I've had of
what's commonly called success, it never occurred to me to
find a word for that time of silence, upheaval, and madness,
that time when hour after hour would go flying by without
our even noticing, when some of my intellectual men friends
cast fearful glances in our direction, what brazenness, their
panic-stricken eyes said, what brazenness, they kiss each
other on the beach, they embrace each other, they laugh,
they run, they say silly things, because the fact is that men
like that are always in a great hurry to define the indefinable,
they need to underline it in heavy pencil, those two are having an affair, they're sleeping together, because those are all
the words they have in their vocabulary, Mar, and they
couldn't understand, as you yourself said, that we made love
another way, without going to bed with each other, holding
hands and forgetting about everything as we sat on the beach
at the water's edge watching the sea, with our behinds damp
from the wet sand and our feet buried in it, losing track of
the time going by, losing track of the kids as they scattered
from one end of the beach to the other, the kids Ernest took
away from you later, the two of us sharing one of those
prolonged silences of ours, with no need to explain anything
to each other, watching the sea and thinking that perhaps we
were two bodies that all of a sudden were turning into just
one, two bodies that had finally found each other after having wandered like idiots all over some unknown galaxy, two
years have gone by, Mar, and maybe you wouldn't recognize
me now, because I'm a reasonable, sensible woman again and

have gone back to reading books to understand what I don't understand about life, because that time together was all too short and I couldn't go on like that, and besides, you weren't there anymore, you'd gone back to your universe, you felt you were *de trop* in this one, and I couldn't follow you, I'm made of clay and fear too, what had been born with you died inside me, and then came the separation from Ferran, and trying to explain how much I loved him despite everything, realizing that I'd climbed aboard a train that was hurtling on and on without stopping, while he stayed behind there in the station, growing smaller and smaller in the distance, and I remember now the famous discussion about round tables and circumferences, how Ferran tried to explain to you that a round tabletop is a circumference and how you laughed as you said to him, But a round table's a round table, isn't that so?, and you stubbornly clung to your own familiar words while Ferran insisted on using his scientific language, because for one thing he's a theoretician and you're a creature from another galaxy. When I watched the rhythm of your heartbeat after they'd put you on the respirator, when I saw how they were forcing you to breathe, up and down, up and down, when you were already far away, I had two different reactions, the first one to rise up in rebellion against the machine and science because they were forcing you to go on existing when you'd already decided that you were leaving this world, and the second one to be angry with you because you'd left me all alone, and as a result I was going to be forced to stop living and start dissembling again, pretending to be a strong woman when I'm not one, pretending that the separation from Ferran was just a transition period, a transfer point in this miserable life, having thirty lives again, an affectionate mother without a guilt complex, a woman who gives public lectures on feminism, a female who satisfies a male promptly and properly, a friend and confidante listening to confessions of failures I don't really want to hear, and all because you had decided to go away . . .

Yes, two years have gone by now since that day, and nearly three since the first time I saw you, though of course you don't remember it the way I do. How could you possibly! You spoke to me in the train as though you'd known me all your life, something that came quite naturally to you, whereas I was totally taken aback on being addressed that way by a perfect stranger, though I remember you always used to say that people either like or dislike each other instantly—and realized later on that that was a line you'd stolen from Shirley MacLaine in *The Apartment*, who'd spoken it with tears and streaks of mascara running down her face, and when I reminded you of that fact your only reply was, Well, so what?—so anyway, there in the train you eavesdropped on the conversation I was having with my sister about the car Ferran wanted to buy, and you butted in when we decided that maybe a Diane was better than a Renault 4, you said, I remember your words quite clearly, that the best thing would be a Citroën 2 CV, the only thing is you have to be careful to watch the oil gauge, you came right out and said that to my face, and then you just sat there calmly looking out the window again and paying no more attention to me, but I stared at you and thought, What nerve, deep down in my subconscious there's a rule that was drilled into me long ago that says it's not good manners to butt in on somebody else's conversation if you haven't been formally introduced, but all you'd said was that about the oil, and then you just sat there looking at the dusty worn-out countryside around Barcelona, lost in your own thoughts, convinced that you'd said what was necessary and not a word more.

But I kept looking at you and after a while I realized I'd seen you somewhere before. You were a strange hybrid creature, part adolescent and part wild animal perhaps. Your red hair hung straight down and I thought to myself, She looks like a Renaissance pageboy. You know, that terrible habit of mine of pinning labels on people simply on the basis of their physical appearance. Skin like that of a fruit and eyes like a woods at dawn. Your eyes even then seemed to belong to another world, and now that you're dead I understand why. Perhaps what made me fall in love with you was your naturalness, your air of seeming innocence, let's say, that insouciance of yours that had both its perverse and its childish side. You aroused a new feeling in me that I was unable to define at the time, a feeling that perhaps lay buried in the darkest corner of my innermost self. A feeling I was in no way inclined to reveal to anyone, least of all Ferran. People thought of me as the sensible woman who gave feminist lectures, who was capable of diagnosing what was wrong with women these days, the spider web, possessing and being possessed, feeling disparaged and devalued from the day we're born, and you know, all the rest of it. But you used to wait for me after I'd given my talk, and you never had one word to say as to whether I'd been brilliant or clever, you simply waited for me in the battered Mehari that was falling apart, put it in gear, and set off in fits and starts to take me far away, perhaps to look at the sea from one of Barcelona's polluted beaches, sitting amid empty Coca-Cola bottles, rusted tubes, and old rope sandals half buried in the sand. There was no need for me to talk too much, or invent a new self, or anything like that, because I wasn't afraid anymore when I was with you, afraid of revealing myself as I really am, that adolescent that I'm continually forced to bury in the dank abysses within myself. And I began to admire you, because, you know, I can't love a person unless it's someone I admire—you weren't like me at all in that respect—I began to admire you as though I were a man and you a crude, unfinished product, with no sophistication whatsoever. With you I left behind me books and theories, the sound reasoning that had led me to conclude that the best way to live is as a liberated woman, though I nonetheless continued to live within the narrow confines of thoughtful reflection, a coward in the face of my impulses and desires, relying solely on my recognized role as a *femme savante* whom everyone expects to come up with the right answers. Yes, I know, those were the wrong rules to be following, but the truth of the matter is that I just didn't know how to love the way you did, I had to put a price on everything, if I give you this much today I want you to give that much back to me tomorrow, a continual tit for tat, whereas you gave all of yourself without even thinking about it, perhaps because you came from another galaxy. Your spontaneity was not the end product of a successful rebellion against any and every attempt to dominate you. You simply exuded naturalness from every pore of your body; your behavior had nothing in common with the studied, snobbish pose of the anti-bourgeoisie. And perhaps my love for you was born of a deep-seated envy at not being like that myself, at not being you, because love is sometimes born of envy. You hadn't broken away from any pattern for the simple reason that you didn't have one in the first place. And I soon came to believe that you had descended from another planet, because otherwise it was impossible to understand how you could live as you did, without ever asking yourself questions about what you were doing, without any theories whatsoever, without ever having thought about the repression you'd been the victim of when you were a child, talking about how happy you'd been when you were little, putting into practice, point by point, our feminist theories, those theories that the rest of us never just go ahead and apply because we're so afraid and so resentful. You laughed when I told you that you were a feminist without realizing it, you sat and listened patiently when I talked to you about how much I admired intelligence and culture, about how it was precisely these two things that had fascinated me most about Ferran, and you jokingly asked me, with an edge of sarcasm in your voice, isn't it possible that you love Ferran because you're so eager to have somebody who's your intellectual equal to keep you company?

Yes, you awakened a telluric force in me, a power at once magical and profound, which may not have been your doing at all, it may have been another link in the infinite lost chain, the chain formed by all those silent grandmothers and great-grandmothers who buried their complaints and their secret pleasures between the walls of a loneliness they never set down in writing. I discovered that when I saw you in the hospital surrounded by all those tubes, an inert body being forced to breathe because of decisions made in the name of scientific progress. And how I hated you at that moment for having left me alone, for having forced me to bury once again what you had awakened in me, what you never ought to have awakened.

You got off the train and it was then that I remembered who you were, who the young woman with skin like that of a fruit and eyes like a woods at dawn was. I placed your image in its proper context, in the public square of the dank town near Barcelona that we lived in. You were the chick whose ass showed when you bent down to button your kids' coats before they got on the school bus. You were wearing carrot-colored boots that came halfway up your thighs and a very short skirt. Then I heard a voice whisper in my ear, That one's a brazen hussy, somebody who pointed her finger at you, a filthy pig and a brazen hussy, the voice repeated. She lives with her husband and a lover, all three in the same house and the same bed. I looked to see who it was that was talking to me and discovered it was the Millionairess. And I answered, in a haughty tone of voice, stories like that don't interest me in the slightest. I was lying, I know now that I was lying. But I was playing to the hilt my role as a discreet

and reasonable intellectual, a faithful reflection of my up-
bringing and education in a fashionable Barcelona suburb,
and it didn't surprise me when I found out later that the Millionairess decided then and there that I was a thoroughly disagreeable person. I thought it over and came to the conclusion that perhaps what separated me from the Millionairess
were certain class differences. I could defend a brazen hussy
and a filthy pig who lives with her husband and her lover in a
disgusting *ménage à trois*, but I couldn't bring myself to
trade gossip with a woman whose whole life was centered on
vulgar rumor-mongering. The fact is that Ferran and I had
decided to live in that dank town in the midst of the lowest
of the low, the *lumpen* of the *lumpen*, because of our socialist
ideas, but doubtless our ideas were nothing more than abstract concepts, and at the time I didn't realize that such a
thing as an impenetrable barrier existed between us and them,
quite apart from money and from ideas, the barrier of language. The Millionairess' gossip-mongering and tale-bearing
played a very important role in her life; it was full of stories
about other people, yet these stories in no way broadened her
horizons. But I, on the other hand, belong to that class of
people who manage to convince themselves that gossip is culture, that it is a very clever way of becoming involved in
things that are really none of their business. And perhaps
that's the reason why Ferran and I left that dank town, for
there was no way of reconciling our preconceived ideas and
the behavior of people such as the Millionairess, people whose
actions were motivated by an odd mixture of kindness and
maliciousness, who never asked themselves *why* they acted as
they did and not some other way. You of course were a
friend of the Millionairess', despite the fact that you were
well aware that she called you a filthy pig and a brazen
hussy, because you knew the Millionairess was unhappy, that
she was unhappy because she was only twenty-one years old
and the Millionaire had gotten her pregnant for the third
time—an insufferable swaggering braggart of a husband who

earned a few miserable pennies a day doing piecework and blew half a day's wages every Saturday night in a bar, treating anybody and everybody in the place to a round of drinks on him. You knew that the Millionairess was slowly dying of disgust and depression at wiping her two little kids' bottoms and their snotty noses all day long in her apartment decorated with horrid Japanese paper flowers, or else sitting in the midst of her three-piece living-room suite surrounded by brats whose yelling and screaming set her every last nerve on edge. It took me a long time to tumble to the fact that the Millionairess' one distraction was telling me what a filthy pig and what a brazen hussy you were because you lived with your husband and your lover, all three of you sharing the same house and the same bed.

When I first saw you, you struck me as being an odd mixture of a girl from a good family and a prostitute-"hostess" in a cheap bar. You were the center of the world, and at the same time you knew how to escape people's notice, surrounding yourself with that air of calm self-possession that only those who have inherited wealth have—those who have spent years and centuries polishing the façade they present to the world. Nonetheless, I soon realized that you unconsciously aroused men's sensuality. You were amoral without even realizing it. And perhaps that's the reason why many women thoroughly hated you: She's a seductress, they used to say to me. Perhaps because you gave the impression of getting whatever you wanted, without any sort of inner conflict or struggle. You really gave yourself, wholly and completely, to a man, and the next day you loved another one just as intensely. You never hid anything. Ferran used to say to me, She's a woman through and through, too much so, and all I could say in reply was that you were the only person I knew who didn't know what jealousy was, that you didn't want to be possessed and at the same time had no idea what it meant to want to possess someone else.

Following that conversation with the Millionairess, when I

earned myself the label of a thoroughly disagreeable person, I
hadn't thought about you again. Until that day on the train,
the day you butted into the conversation and put in your
two cents' worth about 2 CVs and oil. And now that I think
about it, I realize that our relationship was based on movement: it began there in the train and ended that night of the
accident, the night that you went off alone in your battered
Mehari that was about to fall apart. What the two of us had
together was an endless series of concentric movements, like
a spiral forcing us to go farther and farther, without precau-
tions or thought for the morrow. My relationship with Ferran was different, and you never did anything to interfere
with it. My relationship with Ferran was static and calm, but
he was the one who couldn't bear the way you and I moved
along together, our headlong advance toward some point that
lured us irresistibly onward. Toward madness perhaps? Perhaps.

I remembered you as I climbed the stairs at the train station: so then, that chick with the skin like that of a fruit was
the brazen hussy of the town we lived in . . . You doubtless
remember that later on I called you my galactic hussy, or my
whore, and the word filled my mouth with a strange taste, at
once bitter and sweet, because when I said it I became once
more a young lady violating some sort of taboo. That happened when I told you what the Millionairess had said about
you, I thought you'd be angry but you burst out laughing,
ha, ha, ha, that's really funny, I'm the town hussy and filthy
pig, and then you repeated the word I'd used, once, twice, a
hundred times, whore, whore, whore, we're both whores,
you decided. Yes, but you're more of a whore than I am, I
shot back; that's altogether true, you said, because you pass
yourself off as an intellectual, that is to say a hypocrite; come
on, I said, how come you have this thing about intellectuals?,
and suddenly you turned serious: It's you intellectuals who
are always trying to prove that it's all the rest of us who re-

ally live, and then there's that damned mania of yours for finding an explanation for everything . . . Okay, I conceded in a conciliatory tone of voice, I'm a whore inwardly and you're one outwardly, how's that? I don't know, I don't know, you replied, but you soon forgot the whole thing, either changing the subject or else just sitting there not saying a word, and I went on: Do you know what?—even when I'd reached the age of fifteen I still turned as red as a beet whenever anybody uttered the word *whore*, and as I remember I was around thirteen when I saw the word chalked on a wall with all its paint flaking off and ran away as fast as my legs could carry me. And yet there I was, savoring the word *whore*, that word that it would never have occurred to me to say in front of Ferran, not ever, though I might possibly have used the word *prostitute*, or if I were showing off my erudition, the recherché *meretrix*, which reminded me of *genetrix* or *imperatrix*, and perhaps in front of my grandmother I would have said *harlot* or *lady of the evening* or *cocotte*, a word that called to mind the Paris of the Belle Epoque and oysters in the Place Pigalle . . .

I no longer recall either when or how I met you again. It may well have been on one of those deadly dull afternoons when I felt so lethargic I could scarcely move and was waiting with a great long inner yawn for Ferran to come home. It seems to me we ran into each other at the school bus and looked at each other as your kids pulled at your skirts and my kids tugged at mine. I'm sure we looked like two dogs warily sniffing at each other. I don't remember which of the two of us first started walking up a muddy path leading over the hill, as though meeting each other like that again were nothing at all out of the ordinary. I scarcely remember a word being spoken between us, but I do remember very well that all of a sudden I found myself sitting with all the children in the Mehari. It was a great treat for our flock of kids when you headed for the woods, even though it was getting dark. It turned out to be a domesticated woods, full of sickly drooping pines amid underbrush and heaps of refuse. You drove unhurriedly, not at all afraid at the wheel, your eyes staring off into the distance and your left hand holding on to the door that kept falling open every so often. The other door was tied shut with a length of rope. You drove along calmly and confidently, but it also seemed as though you were fleeing from something. Feeling half carsick from all the bouncing and jouncing, I looked at you out of the corner of my eye and saw your face in the shadows, emitting a strange, almost magical force. It seemed to me at that moment to be a hard and violent face, perhaps because of the color reflecting off your skin, which changed from indigo to black all of a sudden. You had a strong chin and eyes staring off in the distance at some strange point that I couldn't make out; all I could see was the drooping pines covered with the dirty gray grit of the outskirts of Barcelona. Once inside the car, you were transformed, your body became much more resilient, with a power and a gracefulness that easily passed unnoticed when you had your two feet on the ground. Danger made you invulnerable. One day, you told me, you said to me: You know what? I'd like to die this way, without turning around, staring straight ahead. But I sat there clinging for dear life to whatever I could catch hold of as everything there inside the car tottered and the kids were thrown one on top of the other like so many empty sacks, and all I could hear was the lot of them laughing and shrieking and clapping their hands, because they were on a safari through the jungle, they said, and the clatter of loose tools banging together. The car seats bounced up and down and the Plexiglas window panels shivered as the Mehari rattled along. Everything seemed to have begun a frenzied dance there inside the woods as the first shadows of night fell. I looked at your profile in the semi-darkness, a lunar profile and a crystal cheek in the shape of an apple. You seemed to have stepped out of the night, or the sea, and the thought came to me that you were like Calypso, emerging from the solitude of your island to meet me again. And it was then that I swore not to say a word about it to Ferran.

We sat down outside the bar at the top of the hill. A long time went by, full of silent pauses and half-words as the day died, leaving behind it a fiery-red cloud blanketing the whole valley. It didn't take long at all to know everything about you. The memories of your childhood, the smell of tangerines, the kisses from your father, a wealthy industrialist before he turned into a tramp and a bum. Your memories seemed exactly the same as mine, and yet they were so different! And then when you fell madly in love with the father of your closest girl friend—that handsome engineer who built tunnels and roads. Your description of him naturally included the fact that his hair had turned to silver at his temples—we'd both remembered that romantic detail from the serials we'd devoured in our adolescence—and you also told me of course how you lost your virtue with him, in a wind tunnel where they were testing jet engines. You told me the whole story in the same monotonous tone of voice, as though you were reciting a litany, and it didn't seem at all dramatic to me that your father had turned out to be a tramp or that you'd been seduced in a tunnel that reeked of tar and gasoline, amid a distant roar of engines that reminded you of bluebottle flies buzzing. And you scarcely even laughed when you told me about your husband, who was also your cousin, a dimwitted sluggard with religious scruples who later went mad on account of what happened to his uncle on his mother's side, a flashy high-stepper who'd kicked off from an attack of angina while he was making it with a virgin in a whorehouse. Only you called it a "fainting spell," if I remember correctly. And you told me how you'd gotten married with the dimwitted sluggard of a cousin with religious scruples because your family forced you to after the story of

the seduction in the tunnel, and more than the story itself
what I remember is that you told it to me as you slowly
sipped a Schweppes through a pink straw. And what I
remember best now is the pink straw and the smell of pines,
and perhaps your lunar profile, and the way in which you
told me the oddest things as though they were not in the least
out of the ordinary, like the business about your husband
going mad when he took it into his head that if he made love
with you he'd die of an attack of angina like his uncle
Claudio, that was the name of the flashy gay blade of an
uncle who had exposed the family's good name to ridicule
and dishonor. And then you told me the part about wearing
dainty, exciting nighties because you didn't realize that your
husband was terrified, but that just made his obsession worse,
and at night in bed he would scream "murderess!" at you and
pull the covers up to the tip of his nose. You scratched your
cheek with the pink straw as you went on with your story,
telling me next about how you paraded around in front of
him in a sexy short nightie, baring first one thigh and then
the other as he lay trembling underneath the covers, because
you couldn't get it through your head that Ernest, your husband and cousin, was in really bad shape. And when you saw
that he couldn't get over being scared to death, you went to
see his father confessor, a silver-tongued Jesuit who consoled
you and tried to seduce you, but didn't go any farther than
that, as you realized a long time afterward, perhaps when
your husband was cured of his mania by a psychoanalyst.
And I don't know why I'm remembering all these things just
now, they're coming back to me all mixed up and confused,
maybe because it's two years now since you went away, and
a little more than three years since that day when you sat sip-
ping your Schweppes through a pink straw outside the bar
on the top of the hill in a fiery twilight and the two of us
smelled of pine and your lunar profile stood out clearly,
glowing with an almost milk-white light. And you told me

how your husband was cured of his obsession about dying during intercourse thanks to the psychoanalyst but how at the same time you for your part lost all desire to make love with him, and there was no way of getting it back, you told me in a very impersonal tone of voice, as though you were recounting the story of some other woman, and perhaps that was what surprised me most about you, not the story itself, nor your husband's terror, nor the attempt of the smooth-talking priest to seduce you, but your matter-of-fact way of telling me all that, since ordinarily we women love to turn our lives into a great drama so as to be understood by everybody in the world!

We scarcely said one word to each other all the way home. The children were dripping with sweat, happy and half-asleep, and the only sound to be heard was the tools banging against each other. You dropped me off at my house and I wanted to introduce you to Ferran, even though I could easily predict his reaction when he saw you, he would half-close his eyes and gently shrug his shoulders as he decided that you were no doubt my latest discovery. But neither he nor I knew at the time that you were going to leave much more than a superficial imprint on me, something that is going to be hard for me to erase, even though I know that what I once felt is dead and done with now, and perhaps neither he nor I had any idea what you were about to set off in me, mad, unexpected reactions that he could never have put up with.

And perhaps the best thing about you was that you arrived on the scene precisely when you should have, at just the right moment to bring about a harmonious reconciliation of time and space, when something inside me was dying, the end of a long period of clandestine struggle under Franco's regime, side by side with Ferran, proud of being an exemplary couple, devoting my life to history, dismissing our daily lives together as unimportant, proud, both of us, of not having the time to love, or to explore together anything that lay deeper than what the immense love that we said we felt for all of mankind demanded of us. Later everything was to fall to pieces and lie scattered all about, tremendously difficult to put back together. And, you know, when Ferran finally left home, it didn't make me miss you that much more, because he left a special emptiness in my life, and you're the only one who can really understand this, since you were the one who taught me that the cliché that has it that one nail drives out another is utter nonsense . . . No, you weren't like all the others. You were ahead of your century, you lived our theories, and perhaps that was the reason why I refused to recognize that defenseless body that they were forcing to breathe by artificial means, I didn't want to say goodbye to that mouth hanging open like an idiot's, to those eyes that no longer peered at me through narrowed eyelids, to those hands dangling clumsily at your sides, I didn't want to say goodbye to the doll that they showed me behind the immaculately clean glass panels of the intensive-care unit, the doll that they were indecently forcing to live with their tubes and their machines. Because even though you were still breathing, even though the respirator registered every single one of your heartbeats, one after the other, you had decided that you couldn't live with us, you had decided to return to your galaxy. And perhaps I hated you because you were forcing me to go on thinking about what we ought to be without my really living it, because once again they'd left me no choice. And the fact is that you managed to do something that none of the men that I loved ever had, you taught me to make love with things, day by day, and awakened in me the first tender shoots of a new woman that I have now buried again. So I introduced you to Ferran, and the two of you just stood there as though you'd fallen into a stupor, not knowing what to say, and then finally you bent down to pick up my cat and she ran away; I wanted to catch her again so you could pet her as much as you liked, but you said leave her alone, cats only like to be loved when they need it.

Little by little I found out other things about you. That you had decided to live alone, just you and your kids, shortly after your husband had been cured, but that he refused to go along with that, because he didn't understand why you should want to do a thing like that, now that he was well again and had gotten over the trauma of his uncle kicking off in the whorehouse, now that he wanted you again. Baby doll, sweetie, he would say to you, shall we play with each other for just a little while? And you would play with him, for just a little while, but then you would feel a tremendous urge to run away. You told me that it was Ernest who had finally gone off, but with an expression on his face that scared you, as though to say: you'll pay for this. And so I soon realized that what the Millionairess had told me about you, that you lived with your husband and your lover, all three of you sharing the same house and the same bed, wasn't true at all. I liked what you told me about your husband-who-was-also-your-cousin before he went away, the part about his loving you so much that he was capable of murder so as to keep you close to him, or when he said to you, If only you became permanently paralyzed so that I could take care of you, I'd take you everywhere in a little wheelchair, baby doll. And you didn't see Ernest's face as he looked at you through the glass, his satisfied, ecstatic expression. I couldn't bear the way he looked at your defenseless body, with eyes that drilled straight through you, ferret's eyes. I was furious at not being able to tell you about that expression on his face as he looked at you. We would have had such a good laugh over it.

Then came the part about the stake, I don't know if you remember. You'd already begun to make your escape, despite the fact that Ernest had gotten over his crisis very nicely and wanted to fuck with you day and night, but naturally he couldn't catch you. You began to look at things around you as though for the first time, things were born just for you and you looked at them intently so as to store them away in your memory, deep down inside you. But you'd go back home even though you could scarcely bring yourself to go inside, the first day you had a terrible scare, something brushed against your face, something rough, and it turned out that your husband had hung strings of garlic all over the house. Ernest thinks I'm a vampire, you told me, he sleeps with a stake alongside the bed, he's certain that I'm going to turn into a female Count Dracula at midnight. He's going to put it through my heart anytime now. But Ernest's fits of madness came over him only at night, so it was easy for him to convince everybody that you were the one who was crazy, a mother who couldn't take proper care of her children, eating at odd hours, dirty shoes and torn jackets, pants held together with a safety pin, and all that was true, but it's also true that I've never seen such happy, noisy, sassy kids, little acrobats who cuddled up next to their mother's generous body whenever they felt like it, and then off the next minute to climb the tallest tree and recite the story of Sinbad and the princess at the top of their lungs. You didn't realize that Ernest held all the winning cards, that his temporary depression brought on by the business about his uncle's death in a whorehouse and all the rest didn't count, nor the fact that at night he believed you were a vampire and wanted to drive a stake through your heart, none of that counted, Mar, and you sized up the situation all wrong, you couldn't see what was coming, you didn't have it in you to have doubts about the future, it never occurred to you that Ernest is a respectable family man during the day, a hard worker and well-off financially, that he now keeps his kids as neat and tidy as children of their class should be.

And you went on telling me your new experiences after that, as though they didn't belong to you either, but it never crossed my mind that you were going farther and farther away from me, I simply thought you were living a different life now, just as I was with Ferran, though he didn't understand, you know, and I really have no idea whether Ferran left me because you set me to dreaming, or rather to daydreaming, and he didn't know what to make of my new personality that was so out of touch with reality, and my house began to be a mess too, my kids learned to climb trees with yours, to act out the story of Sinbad and the princess, to sleep all piled up together in the same bed, to go on safari in your Mehari that kept getting grimier and stickier by the day, full of torn newspapers, lengths of rope, tools that had gotten rusty in the rain, empty Coca-Cola bottles, greasy rags, gasoline stains, doors that kept falling open, broken windows, your Mehari hopping like a toad up the dusty hill, to the knoll that was not conducive to dreaming, with its pines that were slowly dying, their trunks half rotted away and spooky birds the color of ashes perched in them. The kids jumped up and down and did somersaults inside the car and stuck their little peters through the cracks in the plastic body to see who could piss the farthest. And I remember thinking that you were like the Mehari, Mar, terribly hospitable and terribly transitory. I would have liked to abandon my habit of dressing like a schoolgirl from a fashionable Barcelona suburb and wear the same sort of clothes you and your kids did, socks of every color under the sun, jeans faded from being washed so often with bleach in the laundry water, checked shirts with the tails hanging out, big bulky sweaters with such wide shoulders that all of you looked as though you had a hump on your back, or two or three. But the rags and tatters and the safety pins, the humps and the ripped seams made you look even prettier, if that's possible, even more the defiant rebel. And your profile was more lunar than ever when you curled up in a ball on the sofa to listen to Chopin's Second Piano Concerto, with your eyes closed as

though you were already dead. You didn't care for rock
music, you never looked at TV, you hardly ever read a book,
just hours and hours listening to Chopin, perhaps you'd already begun making your escape from this world. And you
used to say to me, your hands gently fondling the steering
wheel, your eyes staring straight ahead like the figurehead of
a ship, as you made your way into the decrepit, foul-smelling
beauty of the ruined woods, you used to say to me, If I have
to die, I want it to be like this.

The first time I visited your house, I hardly recognized
you in the photograph on the wall, a little photo held in place
with thumbtacks. I saw that it was a picture of a couple, the
man had a tie on and hair all slicked down with brilliantine
and that certain smile of a happy and contented male, and
alongside him was a young girl with the face of an anonymous neighbor in a big apartment building. Your hair was a
mass of frizzy curls drawn up in a topknot, in the fashion of
the sixties, and you looked much shorter in the photo than
you really are. The curves of your body were plump and
full, giving fair promise of a future when you'd be downright
fat. You were gazing at the man at your side with the
enthralled look of a woman who has recently fallen in love,
and that was only natural, since the man in the photo was the
dimwitted sluggard of a cousin with religious scruples who
had agreed to marry you after you'd been deflowered by the
father of your closest girl friend in a tunnel where they were
testing jet engines. And that happened a long time before
Ernest called you a murderess after the trauma that he under-
went because of the death of his uncle Claudio, long before
everything. And you began to flee from the house, but not
on account of the strings of garlic or the stake, you began to
flee because the young woman with plump curves and very
frizzy hair had already been deeply buried, you'd buried her
without devouring the books that I had had to devour so as
to understand a little, and I still don't understand anything,

and perhaps that's the reason why I hated you that day with the tubes and loved you at the same time, because you had understood long before I had how a person has to live. I remember now that you often came home late, one day because we'd gone off to the hilltop and the next because you'd gone off with the Argentine. The one who taught you the joys of love, skillfully and unhurriedly, playfully. You were a willing pupil, despite the fact that he was ten years younger than you and that his one ambition was to be a sailor for the rest of his life, which didn't trouble you in the least. You learned to look at a man's body as though it were a river flowing endlessly by, and if a woman cares to she can drink her fill of its waters and walk the tightrope between love and death, and naturally you were such a good pupil that soon you could find no incentive to make it with Ernest, you compared, and that is the beginning of the end of any relationship, or at least any exclusive one. The Argentine youngster who had taught you how to love your own body by way of his, perhaps because you learned how to linger on his shores and listen to his sweet words, which may not have been eternal but nonetheless were not ephemeral, went away one day and you told me how you'd learned to look at yourself in the mirror, in a different way, without stopping to think whether your dress was becoming to you or not or whether your hairdo was perfect, no, since that time it was altogether different, you learned to value the way your body was formed, because it was your body you loved it, you took the time to really look at every last bit of it, including your moist, generous cave, the folds and creases that distended with the promise of pleasure, without fear of being gotten the better of, because you soon learned that a woman never loses anything during a night of lovemaking when she knows why she's giving herself to a man. The Argentine went away and you thought that you were still a novice as far as lovemaking was concerned, so you went off with Joaquim. Or was that after the music teacher? I don't remember very well and it hurts that you're not here to help me get it all straight. Maybe he was before, because Joaquim was jealous of Ernest and you didn't want to leave your husband, the very thought made your heart ache. You spent lots of evenings with Joaquim, helping him fix up the bar, and it seemed as though your life had a meaning in those days: somebody had to give Joaquim a helping hand, because he didn't have a cent to his name and had lived the most miserable sort of existence imaginable, eaten alive by lice when things were so bad just after the war, learning all sorts of difficult trades and accepting all kinds of terrible jobs in order to survive. You were really serious about wanting to help Joaquim, that youngster with the careworn face and shiny hair, so serious that I almost lost track of you altogether, though you did turn up one night with a bunch of wild flowers, perhaps so I'd forgive you, and you curled up next to me to listen to Chopin. Ernest would stay at home waiting for you, carefully preparing supper and putting up strings of garlic. And meanwhile you were spending your evenings hanging pictures, sawing shelves, painting the stairwell leading to the bar. You didn't do men's work in order to prove you were their equal or to show them that you knew how to do the things they did, but simply because you liked that sort of work. You weren't taking your revenge on anybody when you rode around on a motorbike or drove your Mehari at breakneck speed. You knew all about electric plugs and washing machines, and you knew exactly how the pistons in your car engine worked. That world that always seemed magic to me was child's play to you, but at the same time you were as fragile and delicate as glass and maybe that's why certain women hated you and men were afraid of you. Joaquim soon vanished, perhaps because he was jealous, because it was hard for him to understand why you went on living with Ernest, and then the music teacher, half Swiss and half Catalan, appeared on the scene, falling madly in love with you, like in the movies, and for a few days you went around lost in the clouds, with a hollow feeling in the pit of your stomach, your eyes gazing off into I don't know what infinite expanses, and reciting in a monotonous voice poems by Aleixandre written in his old age. And as Ernest left by the front door of your house, dreaming of the happy day when you would at last have become a hopeless paralytic, the music teacher came in through the other door and passed through your life in exactly the same way that Joaquim had before him. And it wasn't that you had a mania for collecting men, you believed that every person has his own story, and the music teacher's story was that he'd just had a terrible disappointment in love that had left him half out of his mind, he'd fallen in love with an impossible dream, you were aware that all you were for the music teacher was a transfer point on his journey toward his final destination: forgetting, and despite your knowing this, you taught him everything you'd learned with Joaquim and the Argentine, and you had no sense of loss or feeling of failure when the music teacher told you he'd fallen head over heels in love with a marvelous young girl and was going to introduce you to her immediately, you simply clapped your hands for joy and kissed him. The music teacher then went into the whole routine, I'll always be grateful to you, how can I ever forget you?, and all the rest of it, words that seemed to you to be freshly minted and touchingly beautiful. The two of you made love together in front of the fire, with great tenderness, you told me. I don't know if you remember that I asked you whether you hadn't felt cheated, if the music teacher's story and the fact that he was leaving you for one of those young things with silky skin and the body of a gazelle hadn't left you feeling hurt and aggrieved. You had no idea what I meant, you had no idea what it was like to be possessive, you loved people in a strange way that had nothing at all to do with the way people love each other nowadays. The only thing you asked of people was that they really and truly love you when they were with you, and that your presence be the center of everything at such times. And you told me in a reproachful tone of voice that those of us who are intellectuals and artists deliberately choose what will cause us suffering in life, that we persist in idealizing what we don't have, that we don't know how to live. And I realized that I was coming down to earth again, laden with signs and symbols to survive failure, that I wasn't like you, that you belonged to some other century. When you were with my men friends, you stubbornly refused to say one word. When they began discussing ideology, you took off for your planet. Everything slips off Mar like water off a duck's back, they would say to me, she's really a strange chick. They said that because there was no way of pinning any sort of label on you, and you know how hard that is to forgive. More than your words it was your actions that bewildered them, something they would define as continually contradictory behavior, they could never predict what role you'd choose to play, and so you escaped the neat pigeonhole they had assigned you in their minds. But very early on I noted a far-off look in your eye, and began to suspect that you had chosen the path that would allow you to flee this world altogether. You hardly ever told me anything about your past, only that your mother's greatest interest in life was her needlework and that your father was a bum wandering about the streets of the town. The smell of tangerines reminded you of a man with rough hands who fondled you and eyes with streaks of red all around pupils that stared at you intently. You knew that your father was a tramp who roamed about collecting old newspapers or rummaging through garbage cans like a cat in the night, and you pictured him in your mind as a tall shadow disappearing from sight in the stretches of darkness between the lampposts along the streets of the town. My father has a green face, you used to say to me, and when I wanted to know why your father had a green face you were already somewhere else. Perhaps you were searching for an image of your father in all the men you loved, I don't know.

During those two years I persuaded myself that with me you weren't trying to escape. When we took long leisurely walks together, losing our way in the maze of winding streets in the old sections of Barcelona, mingling with the crowds, with men, when I put my arm across your shoulders, feeling once again the adolescent pleasure of violating a taboo. When we brazenly drank out of the same glass of wine in front of the startled waiter, or pretended that you were a secretary and I was a film producer who was out to seduce you. They say that happy people are all alike and have no story, but I don't think that's true at all. I was happy with you and those moments are still there, faded by time, motionless at certain times and moving at others, but in any event still there, turned now into a painfully acute nostalgia and impossible to forget. These moments appear before me as seemingly useless odds and ends and bits and pieces, it hurts to put them together, and the adolescent I once was who'd gone away, whom you suddenly and unexpectedly brought back, refuses to believe that the past will never return. We pretended we were Esther Williams in your antique bathtub with the rusty edges and the dragon's feet, we imitated Gilda singing that part that went Lover of mi-i-i-ine, I love you so-o-o-o-o, you don't know how mu-u-u-uch, you'll never kno-o-o-o-ow, both of us wrapped up in the same big bath towel that you'd swiped in a fancy hotel you'd stayed at when you went on a trip with Ernest, passing a cigarette in a long holder back and forth between us or imitating an interminable gloomy dialogue from a Bergman film. Then we acted out the scene between the secretary and the movie producer, the two of us standing in front of the gleaming white tile wall. "That's an adorable dress you're wearing, my dear," ". . . do you like it?" ". . . yes, but I like what's inside it even more," ". . .

well, a woman has to be careful about her looks, you know,"
(lowering your eyes at this point the way Marlene does was
an absolute stroke of genius) ". . . and your skin is as soft as
a young girl's," (my fingers barely touched your arm and
you seemed to shiver) ". . . oh, I bet you tell that to all the
girls," ". . . but with you it's different, you're a woman with
class, moreover, my wife is such a bore . . . It would please
me if you came up to my apartment with me, I always have a
bottle of champagne on hand there for very special occasions," ". . . oh, darling, I'd adore to . . ." And we went
back out into the night in your Mehari, on the prowl for vic-
tims, who weren't hard to find. There was always some
would-be seducer who would drive up right alongside us,
lean his elbow on the windowsill of his car, and make a
lightning-quick calculation as to exactly what his chances
were in the few seconds or so before the traffic light turned
green. As the Don Juan in question sized us up, we would
give him come-hither looks, and just as he decided he had it
made, you would put your foot to the floor, accelerating
hard, whip the Mehari around his car, and tuck in right in
front of him as we stuck our tongues out at the frustrated
seducer, and that was the worst insult of all, since it was un-
forgivable for two women, both of them past thirty, to play
cat-and-mouse without observing even the most basic rules of
the game. And to tell the truth we never thought of it as
being a thirst for revenge. No, it was impossible to imagine
you feeling any sort of urge to get even with men. You had
already passed the stage of hating men and were simply
yourself. And there was no use in my continuing to theorize
about feminism in my lectures, racking my brains to find
some plausible way out of the entire historically conditioned
mess, talking about the oppression that our unconscious pose
as castrating, fearful, resentful creatures had brought upon
us, because you just calmly went about getting your way
with men, whereas I on the other hand lay awake all night

unless I took two or three sleeping pills, and cried and cried every morning in the shower, trying to get over being separated from Ferran. Yes, that's how you were till Ernest hired a lawyer, up until then men had never been able to get the better of you, Mar, but taking the kids away from you was too much for you, how could you have understood, how could you have foreseen that the cousin you cared so much about was going to react in that way?

The time we had was too short, Mar, too short to realize how happy I was without having to ask myself why. It seemed as though all the pieces of the puzzle had been put back together again, as though each different part of my body had found the proper space for itself again, as though my mind had been reconciled with the universe. During that short year I succeeded in being myself, for the first and last time in my life, and it wasn't only on account of the laughs we had together, or the play-acting we did just for the fun of it, or the affection. Nor was it on account of our secret sense of triumph when men on the street would get all upset at seeing us together and scream "Dirty lesbians!" at us. When we walked along holding each other's hand, a terrible sin, since women are only permitted to walk arm in arm . . . When we gave each other a big hug in the middle of the beach just because we suddenly felt like it . . . When we went out swiping modernistic flowerpots from the pretty houses that had been occupied by summer residents and were deserted now, on freezing-cold moonless nights in the month of cats . . . What sort of love potion did you give me? All of a sudden you looked at me with your eyes of a woods at dawn and said to me: Do you realize how we make love? Do you realize how two women can love each other in a different way from a man and a woman? Of course, I answered. Even though I was terrified of the abyss that was opening up before me, to tell the truth, and you soon noticed, when you proposed that the two of us go north together in your

Mehari. And you kept saying, They don't understand us, and when you said "they" you were talking about a vague, aggressive, anonymous crowd, "they" were the men who could not forgive the fact that we loved each other, that we couldn't define that love in words, that we didn't reserve "it" for them, that we shared what ought not to be shared.

I kissed you only once. It was in the old studio apartment I rented after reading Virginia Woolf's *A Room of One's Own*. I don't have it any more, you know, because after what happened with Ferran all my money vanished into thin air, and since I don't have the five hundred guineas a year of my own that she had it's not possible for me to have a studio of my own. The two of us lay on the Algerian blanket together, worn out from having rummaged through the old and decrepit odds and ends of furniture and miscellaneous trash and junk left behind by the woman who'd rented the place before. It was just shortly before Ernest told you what he intended to do about the kids, just shortly before the accident. We were talking about the old lady who had died all alone in this apartment, buried in piles of newspapers falling apart with age and sacks of garbage lined up in neat rows all over the place. That old woman fascinated us, for amid pairs of outsize, much-mended underdrawers, mother-of-pearl rosaries, heaps of tattered old-fashioned clothes, yellowed missals and gray flannel undershirts, we found her letters and some photographs, along with a moth-eaten fox scarf that you draped around your neck and proceeded to parade up and down the hall waggling your behind. How do I look in it? Like a *cocotte*, my queen. And you and I lived the story of the old woman, who had died in a pool of her own piss and vomit after the last drinking session of her life. The old woman who drinks anisette, people in the neighborhood called her. And by looking through her letters and photographs in which she appeared alongside an elegant gentleman in a broad-brimmed white felt hat, we discovered that they were lovers, and that the gentleman with the broad-brimmed hat had left his wife for her, and the two of them had lived the last years of their lives together. But the gentleman had died first and left her nothing in his will, and the old woman had stayed on alone in the apartment, slowly dying along with all the things around her, the toilet soon stopped working, the faucets all clogged up, the filth accumulated as the old woman was able to gather just enough strength together to go down to the bar on the corner every afternoon as dusk was falling and down one after the other in one swallow three or four glasses of anisette that left a sweet taste in her mouth and reminded her of days long gone, an old woman who'd turned into a slattern, forgotten by the neighbor women and the concierge who complained about the stench coming from her apartment . . . And the yellowed photographs and the letters remained there, amid all the filth and all the junk, the last palpable traces of the life that the old woman had led at the side of the only man she'd loved in her whole miserable life, they remained there for two unknown women who wanted to have a room of their own after reading Virginia Woolf to find and understand a little, understand that insignificant act of a woman who abandoned everything to go off with a man who was one day to leave her nothing in his will. And I think I said to you, Life isn't tragic, it's ridiculous, can you imagine, I talk a lot about feminism and get all choked up like a sentimental fool over this story of "a woman in love who abandons everything for the man in her life." And you didn't answer, you looked at the little glimmers of late-afternoon light filtering through the cracks in the wall on the street side of the apartment with the balcony outside. Then after a while you answered, Such light, just look. That was all you said, that about the light. We were lying on top of the Algerian blanket with your face resting on my belly. Your hair tickled and that was when I kissed you.

And two years have gone by now since you went away, Mar, since that day when you came to my house, all upset and trembling with anxiety, and said to me, Ernest's gone to a lawyer, he's going to take the kids away from me, he says the law is on his side, he's claiming I'm crazy, that I'm not a good mother. And I answered that you had to fight back, that children belong to their mother. I remember your blazing eyes as you shouted at me, Children don't belong to anybody, do you hear, they don't belong to anybody! And that was when you proposed that I go north with you, far away, but you knew that Ernest was going to come out the winner, he had money and a good job and you didn't have anything at all. You proposed that I go away with you, but I didn't want to leap into the abyss, I'd gone as far as the edge of it but I had to go back to my planet, Mar, I had to get back my powers of reason again, to keep on working so as to understand just a little. You left then, slamming the door behind you, and three days later I found out about the accident: your car had gone over a cliff in the Tossas Pass. You'd gone back to your galaxy, Mar, and left me here alone, and for quite a while now I haven't even known what it's like to cry, because when you went away you took tears with you too.

LONELINESS
("Bedidut")

Shulamith Hareven

SHULAMITH HAREVEN *was raised in Jerusalem. Today, married, with two children, her home—both actual and literary—is still in Jerusalem. She was a member of the Haganah Underground, serving as a teenage medic during the siege of Jerusalem. Later, as an army officer, she took care of transitory camps for Jewish refugees from Arab countries in the early 1950s, and was one of the founders of the Army radio station, Galei Zahal. She accompanied her husband when he served in a diplomatic post in Paris in the early 1960s.*

Ms. Hareven is a publicist in the Israeli press and on the current list of opinion-makers.

Shulamith Hareven has published seven books: two of poetry, three collections of short stories, one volume of children's verse, and one novel, City of Many Days. *She has published translations of classical literature into Hebrew from several languages and has also translated dramas which have been presented on the Israeli stage. She is at present the only female member of the Academy of the Hebrew Language; she has been the recipient of several literary prizes.*

Shulamith Hareven sees her work as craft in the medieval sense of the word. Her favorite genre is the short story, through which she depicts psychological portraits of individuals trying to find their place against the highly diversified backdrop of modern Israel.

LONELINESS

("Bedidut")

by Shulamith Hareven

TRANSLATED FROM THE HEBREW
BY HILLEL HALKIN

Mrs. Dolly Jacobus, who in recent years had arrived at a sure and sedate self-love, sat at her desk pondering how to finish a letter. It was a letter to her husband. All morning long she had basked in the fact that he was at an architects' conference in Malta, and that she could write him there, write the word *Valletta*, which had such a light and chivalrous sound that it made her think of a young, robed knight quickly dismounting and elegantly stripping off his riding gloves: Valletta. Not until she had sat down to write did the reality become too much for her: what really did she know about such places, or about the space, proper or outlandish, that Meir Jacobus occupied in them? She could never imagine her husband once she was no longer by his side. Perhaps he had a different existence then, a different face.

Copyright © 1977 by Shulamith Hareven, by special arrangement with Keter Publishing House, Jerusalem.

Mrs. Dolly Jacobus took her pen and continued to write:

It is 10 A.M. now. Lots of light strikes the desk through the branches of the big olive tree. Do you remember how uncertain I was whether you had planned the window correctly? It seemed so high. But I'm glad of it now: there's just the right amount of light at just the right times. It's a lovely house, Meir. When I go to town and come back—and I don't go that often, because it's still been very rainy, and between one rain and the next the whole city is out in the streets trying to catch up on its affairs—it seems to me that someone has been in the house and has managed to slip away while I was still on the stairs. I look in the mirror and try to make out who it was. Perhaps it's a sign that you're thinking of me and the house. If you're planning to bring me a lace scarf from Malta, please bring a golden, white, or ivory one, and, in any event, not black. And since I have no idea how you're managing your time there, let me remind you of the advice that you once gave me: *surtout, pas trop de zèle. Adieu,* my dear friend.

She quickly reread the letter: yes, it would pass muster beneath her husband's finely critical eye. There were no annoying questions in it of the how-are-you? when-are-you-coming back? variety, no burdensome I-miss-you's or it's-so-difficult-without-you's. Meir Jacobus had taught her long ago that an undue concern for the practical arrangements of life was a distinctly plebeian trait. Within a year or two of their marriage she had learned not to ask what would be. What will be, will be, he would quietly answer her. Sometimes, taking pity on her anxiousness, he would add: "In the station that you've reached, Dolly, you can afford to be impractical."

Mrs. Dolly Jacobus took a long envelope, sealed the letter inside it, and addressed it to the hotel in Valletta in a slightly slanting hand. Her handwriting was unusual: the letters were long, tall, personal, somewhat squared at the edges, as though she had practiced developing a private calligraphy of her own. Only her signature was small and crumpled, a shelter within a shelter within a shelter. A graphologist had once frightened her with the opinion that it was a drawing of a fetus in the womb. Four consecutive miscarriages of indeterminable cause left her without children and with the perpetual irritation of an impatient soul that strives for wholeness and cannot understand why it has not come, what can be taking it so long? Only in recent years had this irritation begun to wane. It was with a measure of optimism that she now looked after her home, her husband, and her many flowerpots. She regarded herself in the mirror with a satisfied if slightly critical air. She went to lectures at the university, where she had her favorite professors whom she never missed, and her passing academic friendships with their head-nods across rows of chairs and their between-class banter.

Self-love had descended on her slowly, by degrees; it had grown securely out of that greater, more comprehensive love that she had felt for her beautiful home, her books, her paintings, her expensive shoes that were too elegant to be Israeli, her restaurants, her credit cards (yes, Mrs. Jacobus, of course, Mrs. Jacobus), her view of the walled Old City of Jerusalem on which the windows of her house looked down. Dolly Jacobus considered this view to be a private performance put on in her behalf, which she would watch from her gallery in all its many aspects of time and light. Once a visiting friend from the university had sat at the wide window bathed in Herodean light and asked after a long silence:

"Do you mean to tell me that you can go on looking out on all this every hour of the day without feeling anxious?"

Dolly Jacobus lifted and dropped one shoulder.

"And you can just go on looking down on all this?" the visitor asked again wonderingly. "Just looking down?"

"I must be a butterfly," said Dolly Jacobus. Her face broke into the lopsided grin that helped make her so likable. "But I want you to know," she added, "that being a butterfly is something that I have to work at very hard."

She was too rich for anyone to feel really sorry for her, yet people still said "poor Dolly" when they mentioned her. Nobody knew why. A year before, she had taken up batik and made gifts of her many creations, but the dyeing proved too messy for her and she gave it up in the end. Instead she tried writing haikus. She would in fact have sent her husband a few pithy haikus right now in lieu of a letter, but for her fear that the poems might travel poorly and spoil in the course of their flight over the unnecessarily large ocean that separated her from Meir. All a person really needed in the way of room, she had once thought to herself, was three or four streets around him. Only someone who had never been a refugee could dare dream of oceans and great expanses of space. And twenty-five years ago Dolly Jacobus had been a refugee. To this day she was astonished by such things as central heating which kept on burning warmly, really burning, in a house while the rain remained outside. Truly outside, it wasn't just an optical illusion.

It turned out that she was out of postage stamps, and since she had planned a trip to a delicatessen downtown anyway, she decided to go buy some. Settling into her small car, she reached into the glove compartment and took out a pair of embroidered house shoes in which she preferred to drive. With her feet in the soft slippers, the car itself became a kind of private room. The rearview mirror showed her a pointed, attractive face with the barest hint of—not that she actually had the beginnings of one, but the skin above her lips was a trifle darker than elsewhere, so that in all her photographs she was obliged to have it lightened—a mustache over her upper lip. Dolly adjusted the mirror and turned the key in the ignition. To her satisfaction, the motor started at once despite the cold weather.

The city sped toward her in a rush of confusion. People had trouble deciding whether to open their umbrellas or close them: those who opened them had them blown inside-out like a funnel by the wind, while those who closed them were liable to be drenched by a sudden gust of rain. Both parties hurried impatiently, lengthening a stride to avoid a puddle or shortening one against a blast of wind. The hair of the women blew wildly; here and there a young girl ran giggling to catch her kerchief that had flown away. Dark patches of rain stained the walls of the houses. Blotchy clouds sped through the sky between the roofs, through which at irregular intervals the sun struggled to appear. Some children were sailing a paper boat in a dirty puddle. A gray truck whose driver seemed lost in thought drove right through it, spraying grimy water mixed with bits of paper in every direction. The city stone seemed dim and weary. The whole street smelled disagreeably of wet dog fur. For a minute Dolly contemplated turning back to shelter within the clean, warm comfort of her house with its central heating that burned, really burned, cheerily all the time. But she had already come too far.

She parked in a lot downtown. Meir Jacobus' office was nearby, on the top floor of one of the new sharp skyscrapers that seemed determined in their hatred of the city to get as high above it as they could. No private individual would ever build such a thing for himself; people did such things in groups to get rich quickly from the city. The contracting firm that built this particular building also employed its guards and maintenance staff, as well as the attendants in the nearby parking lot. Once, while having her car washed, it was whispered by one of them in Mrs. Jacobus' ear that the

firm was not on the up-and-up, and even short-changed its
employees in their paychecks. For a while she thought of
doing something about it; after all, people should have a
union that will press their demands. Not that she knew the
first thing about it, far from it, but these were matters that
everyone read about in the newspaper: workers had unions
and even went out on strike. It upset her to see people ill-
treated, and she raised the subject one day in Meir's office. It
was afternoon and she had come to drive him home. His
sister and partner, Bilhah, an architect herself and a triple
divorcee with an exaggeratedly svelte body and a passion for
jewelry, was there too. Almost apologetically, Dolly Jacobus
murmured something about exploitation, about overtime,
something about unions. Bilhah glanced up from her drafting
paper, her bracelets and bangles coolly silent, and said:
"Really, Dolly, I don't know why on earth you should
want to be such a do-gooder."
Dolly didn't want to be a do-gooder. She dropped the subject. Still, something of the good will she felt remained with
her, something of that indefinable sympathy that everyone
can sense even if no one can put a finger on it, so that the
men would smile at her especially and inquire how she was.
Sometimes she would put a question to them herself and get
an answer. She knew, for instance, that the parking-lot attendant on duty today had recently divorced his wife after
no end of tribulations and appearances in court. Now, having
parked according to his directions that bore more resem-
blance to a personal plea, she observed him carefully through
the window, then took a little notebook from her bag and
wrote down:
"The divorced man: his shirt more pressed than usual
(laundries), his shoulders more hunched than usual (restaurants)."
Her notebook and the insight that went into it improved
her mood. She considered herself an astute observer. Dolly

has a keen eye, she often remarked to herself. She snapped her bag shut as the attendant approached the car window. "Good morning, madame, how are you today, maybe you'd like the car washed?" She flashed the broad smile that she reserved for her faithful followers, "No, thank you, the car won't be here long enough, but please don't forget to remind me next time, you know how forgetful I am, really, I don't know what I'd do without you." As she talked, she felt that she was overdoing it, saying and smiling too much. Meir would have gotten the same message across with two words and a short wave of his hand. The attendant too was confused and didn't know whether to stay or leave. Was there something else the lady wished to say to him? Luckily, another car entered the lot at that moment and saved him from his predicament.

Dolly locked the car door and made a mental note to give the man a gift for his politeness on the first available holiday. Indeed, Purim was next week: perhaps some imported deodorant would do. It was a pity how few people in this perspiring land understood the importance of deodorant. Such a gift would be both practical and pleasurable. Yet, Dolly Jacobus was far from a brainless woman: what would happen, she asked herself, when the supply of expensive deodorant was used up? The parking-lot attendant had alimony to pay and certainly could not afford such luxuries, while she and Meir could hardly supply him with deodorant forever; a can every holiday, or perhaps even every week, how absurd. In the meantime the sun reappeared and the clouds in Dolly's mind dispersed too. She would give it to him this once and take her chances. What was so wrong with making a man happy just once? Life was all ups and downs anyway.

Having withstood the temptation to succumb this time too to an undue concern for practical arrangements, which was always a source of anxiety, her mood improved even more.

Dolly Jacobus was an orderly woman who didn't like to leave problems unsolved, not even the bare thought of one. She smoothed out her dress and walked to the building. A silent elevator took her quickly to the top floor, where her husband's office was.

The door was open. Bilhah was inside by herself, bent over some tracing paper with a compass. She was always bent over something. A low desk lamp cast an intense pool of light on the table, in which Bilhah's rings bubbled as though being brought to a boil.

"Oh, it's you," said Bilhah Jacobus unenthusiastically. Her rings fell silent for a moment, then started to bubble again.

"Are you alone? Where's Esther?"

Esther was the secretary, a tall, ugly, unpleasant, gum-chewing girl who wore a wig made of someone else's hair and had never learned to answer the telephone properly. Moreover, she didn't even need the job, nor did Meir and Bilhah really need a secretary; but her parents, of a prominent Jerusalem family that had two or three different marriage ties with the Jacobuses, had pleaded for her.

"Esther has been working so hard all year long," said Bilhah sarcastically, "that she decided to take a vacation. Now that Meir is away, she thought she had one coming to her."

"Maybe she did."

Bilhah threw her a mocking look that left nothing out or unalluded to, from Esther's glum, gum-chewing slow-wittedness, to the niggardly, have-pity-on-me vibrations that she gave off. Before such realities Dolly Jacobus could not but bow down. In Meir's and Bilhah's tolerance of Esther, it seemed to her, was a certain hypocrisy, a kind of mock stoicism that was too much for her to understand.

"What are you doing now, Bilhah?"

"The same as before Meir took off."

"What's that?"

"Entrances for Zone Three of the Jewish Quarter. Didn't Meir tell you?"

Bilhah knew perfectly well that Meir never told her anything.

"Show me."

But Bilhah placed her hand over the paper.

"There's nothing to see yet. You wouldn't understand it anyway."

Each time Dolly felt all over again how out of place she was in this office, which was Meir's workaday world. Whenever she telephoned and was answered by Esther's wooden voice, her depression was so great that she couldn't remember what she had called to say. More than once she had actually forgotten some urgent matter and hadn't dared call back again. It was like standing by a sea rail and watching things fall from one's hands into the water, irretrievable.

"I'm going to the post office now, Bilhah. Is there anything urgent for Meir?"

"Look on his desk," came the indifferent reply. Bilhah returned to her measurements. Two heavy bracelets jangled on her wrist.

Dolly Jacobus went over to the window, which wasn't a real window but an immovable panel of glass. The sight of the bare, unshaded light bulb burning in the broad daylight of the room made her uneasy. There was something abnormal, something hybrid and unlifelike about it, almost a sin against those natural processes that have their own relaxed flow. This dizzying, too high, too enclosed, eternally air-conditioned room with its hermetically sealed windows and its strong lamplight at eleven o'clock in the morning, when a premature spring wind was whirling outside, disturbed her peace of mind and all but depressed her. She felt the need to get outside into the fresh air and leaves. From time to time an unmistakable gust from the south pierced the galloping whirlpool of air, flaring the nostrils with keen desert desire—a southern breeze such as could only be felt in Jerusalem in autumn and spring. To get away, away, to gallop quickly, to give oneself away.

Nothing of this could be felt in the office. Bilhah Jacobus was confined to her white beam of light, from which she declared:

"There's something there from Grandma Haya that Meir hasn't seen yet. She commands us to close the windows in her dining room that face out on the new housing projects. She says that she can't stand to look at them, that each time she sees how they've ruined her mountain, her blood pressure goes up."

There was always some new story about Grandma Haya that was always being told with the same helpless affection. Grandma Haya was a monument, and monuments are a law unto themselves. She was eighty-nine years old, though she confessed to only eighty-seven, and still cooked all her holiday specialties for her daughters-in-law, who—poor things!—had no strength of their own. One time she paid a royal visit to Dolly and Meir's house, where she sat for a long time at the broad window that looked down on the Old City from above. Yes, yes, she said. It all belonged to her. She could look out on it all, she who had never been a young starving refugee with a funny family name that had to be changed in a new land. Grandma Haya appraised Dolly sternly and asked if there were roaches in her kitchen. "No, Grandma Haya, there aren't," said Dolly, hiding a smile. Grandma Haya declared firmly:

"I congratulate you."

Meir and Bilhah's grandmother lived in an old house full of arches with an outdoor toilet that she used day and night, summer and winter, and refused to exchange for a modern, indoor one such as Meir and Bilhah had been begging her to install for years. The rooms of her house were abrasively spotless, cleaner than clean, with their white curtains, whiter tablecloths, and heavy silver candlesticks polished to such a brilliance that they seemed to shine even at night. In his childhood, Meir claimed, he had been afraid to sleep in the same room with the candlesticks because of their light. Each time he awoke, he thought he was seeing a thief's flashlight.

One wall of Grandma Haya's bedroom was covered with a large map of the world in which were stuck little flags. Grandma Haya was a sixth-generation Jerusalemite, she had grandchildren and great-grandchildren all over the globe, and she wanted to know exactly where each one of them was. An orange flag with the name Nurit on it was thrust into London. A bright-blue flag that said Elisha and Tali was near Tel Aviv. There was a reddish flag for Yoav somewhere in Sinai. (Not that Yoav ever served in Sinai, but Grandma Haya assumed that if he was in the army, it could only be there.) She had once been in Sinai herself with her departed husband, the doctor, on an expedition of Englishmen, and had ridden sidesaddle, as was the custom of ladies in those days. Her memories of the trip—more portraiture, really, than memory—were of ravens, cliffs, and untold dangers. Perhaps vague longings for the place lingered on, for why else would she so staunchly insist that Yoav was there when he wasn't, braving all those dangers, especially when she couldn't even recall very well how he looked?

Grandma Haya was distressed that so few of her flags were in Jerusalem, while in the United States alone there were three, one belonging to Adi, who had been married there in a Catholic church. At first Grandma Haya had wanted to pull that flag out of her map, but at the last minute she relented, so that it remained crookedly in place as though it did not quite belong. Dolly clearly remembered the moment nearly twenty years ago when Grandma Haya had risen from her seat, and planted in the heart of Jerusalem a lemon-colored flag that said Meir and Dolly on it. They had already been

married two weeks at the time, but to all of them this seemed
the real wedding. At last Dolly had come home. The bare,
goaty hill outside the window had seemed to her a potential
disaster area of which she alone was afraid. Now that her flag
stood firmly in Grandma Haya's map, she felt that she too
could relax.

Dolly Jacobus stood in her husband's office and pressed her
head against the storm-beaten, forever-sealed window; Bilhah
sat in the strong beam of light silently swearing at some un-
successful calculation, her jewelry coming slowly to a boil
again, and up on her hillside Grandma Haya sat at home, furious at the intruding projects that had put her old age to
shame. For once in her life she too had no strength to fight
back.

There was a long line of people in the post office. The fan
on the ceiling wasn't working. At the head of the line stood a
messenger boy from some office with several dozen registered
letters. As soon as he finished, two soldiers advanced out of
turn and demanded to be served. The post office kept growing more packed; it was as though half the city had decided
to crowd into it, each person with many items to mail. The
clerk at the window was slow and incompetent, complaints
began to be heard. Dolly Jacobus would glady have left, but
she was already nearer to the front of the line than the rear,
and to elbow her way back out through the dense crowd
seemed harder than waiting her turn. Perspiration formed on
her forehead.

Directly in front of her stood a very small teenage girl
with the emaciatedly thin, almost monkeylike appearance of
a stunted child. Only her chest and her buttocks stuck
sharply out like false appendages that didn't quite belong to
her. There was something pitifully sharp and shrunken about
her, as though privation had caused her to stop growing in
the womb; she seemed more a homunculus than an actual

person, a snuffed-out, lightless little candle. A strong smell of the cheapest violet-scented perfume came from her body together with an odor of cigarettes and sweat. No doubt the perfume took the place of daily baths, very likely she slept in her clothes. Amid the great press of people, her curly hair was thrust right beneath Mrs. Dolly Jacobus' nose. She wore tiny doll-like blue jeans that were slightly open at the waist and a purple blouse still shiny from some bargain stand. Where the two failed to meet, a strip of naked, pathetically lackluster skin was exposed, on which grew a dark tuft of animal-like hair. She looked concentrated, smoky, and bad. Her neck was unwashed.

In the girl's hands, Mrs. Jacobus saw, were two registered letters from the law office of Advocate Yitzhaki on Ben-Yehuda Street. Dolly Jacobus and her husband knew Yitzhaki well and had often visited his large home in the German Colony, which somehow made the girl seem less a stranger to her. With her usual avidity to be liked by her inferiors, or perhaps out of a loneliness so habitual that she no longer even sensed that it was there, she smiled encouragingly at the girl. The complaints and congestion had grown worse, if such a thing were imaginable, and Dolly Jacobus sought to free herself of them by moving forward a bit, when she suddenly realized to her astonishment that the dark-skinned waif of a girl not only failed to move too, but deliberately seemed to press backward and turn her head, so that her dark mouth unmistakably delved like an inquisitive kitten's against the soft silk bodice covering Mrs. Dolly Jacobus' right breast. A current of rare flame shot through Dolly's body, and with it, an indistinct fear. She sought to move away once more, which was far from easy in the great throng of people that had long ceased to preserve even the semblance of a line. This time, however, there was no possibility of error: the girl pressed against Dolly Jacobus' stomach again, as though in an open and explicit invitation. She could feel the burning, monkeylike heat of her seemingly chronically feverish body. All of a sudden the girl looked up and regarded Mrs. Dolly Jacobus with a sharp, clairvoyant impudence.

A hot wave, heavy, tropical, and damp passed over Dolly Jacobus. She jerked back her hand so as not to touch the girl's waist and offendedly clamped her mouth shut. Yet she knew, with a weak, sinking feeling, that she could no longer resist the wave of desire rising, illimitably shameless, within her. Not that she was unaware of the element of sadism in this sudden new passion, of her need to trample, to assail. But the girl appeared not to mind, appeared to size up the situation exactly with an omniscience as old as the world. Compared to her, I'm an amateur, Dolly Jacobus thought to herself, a rank amateur. She shut her eyes, conscious that in another moment she would move closer to the knowing little body of her own accord. Just then, however, the post-office manager sent a clerk to open a second window; the line melted away, and the girl stepped forward with her registered letters as though nothing had happened. She mailed them and left the post office without looking at Mrs. Jacobus.

Dolly Jacobus put stamps on the letter to Valletta, which was no longer a knight or even a geographical place but simply a sound. She bought a few extra stamps and dropped the letter in the mailbox, as though glad to be rid of it. When she turned to look for her, the girl had already disappeared among the passersby and been swallowed up by the street. Dolly Jacobus retraced her steps toward the parking lot, entered a dimly lit cafe on the way, drank something hurriedly, and thought that the storm had subsided. Yet when she turned onto Ben-Yehuda Street she felt suddenly so faint, and the slope of the sidewalk seemed so steep, that she feared she would have to negotiate it on all fours. How, she wondered, could everyone else be taking such a precipitous drop in stride? I will never make it to the bottom, she said nearly out loud to herself. Hesitantly she began to walk step-by-step to her car, when she chanced to meet an acquaintance, a tall, merry young student from the university wrapped in a duffle coat against the errant wind, who mercifully accompanied her part of the way. By the time he took his leave with seven-league strides, he left her feeling better, sorry to see him go.

Dolly Jacobus had often wondered about the meaning of home. There were so many homes in the world, so many houses, and out of them all each person had one alone in which he knew where everything was. Of all the hundreds of thousands of homes, she thought, there is one alone to which I have the key and know that in the top drawer of the chest in the bedroom to the left is a tan camel's-hair sweater; of all the impenetrable, anonymous houses there is only one in which I can find right away the set of dishes that Meir brought from Spain. The lighter. The broom. The wash-and-dry sheets. Now, however, as she sat motionless in her car, she was no longer so sure of this nexus of knowledge between her and her house. If she were to return to it this minute, she felt, the key might not fit the door, so that she would remain trapped outside in impersonal space. And if it did fit, her memories might not. The sweater might not be in its drawer, and who knew whether the chest would be there at all; whether a different table would not be standing in place of the one she knew; whether the whole familiar house would not turn out to have been a dream, and the house she returned to a strangely furnished place that she had never arranged. Instead of her rosebushes there might be a strip of concrete on which an electric generator clanked intolerably away. Perhaps a gang of workers. Perhaps the house had been condemned already without her knowing it.

She ran a hand over her forehead to drive the nightmare away. It wasn't the first such ghastly vision she had had in the past two or three weeks. Several times she had dreamed

that a stranger, someone she should have known but somehow was unable to recognize, had broken into her house;
struggling with the hideous, mocking secret of who he was,
she had broken free each time with a choked little cry. Now
she was alone, and it was hard waking by herself in the middle of the night. Often she left the night light on. Yet the
panic underneath remained.

This is no good, Dolly Jacobus said to herself, wonderingly: this is no good. Pulling herself together, she stuck the
key in the ignition and decided to visit Grandma Haya.

If the weather outside was still behaving strangely, none of
it was noticeable in Grandma Haya's house, which had a
weather all its own. Meir had once remarked that Grandma
Haya was the last ecological person in the family. She would
never have dreamed of buying parsley and other herbs; she
grew them herself, planted by the fig tree and the lemon tree
in the courtyard. The idea, Grandma said, of buying a lemon
in a store. The balsam with which she scented her linen closet
was picked by her in the hills, or by one of her grand-
daughters when her back hurt too much to go look for it. An
egg was a meal for her, and who could explain to her, pray,
why people ran around as they did nowadays and caused
themselves all kinds of diseases of the liver and the heart?
People don't live by human proportions anymore, she would
say: they build too high, live too high, and talk too high. It's
an insult to creation. Offices, everyone must have an office.

It was indeed Meir's and Bilhah's good fortune that she had
never been to their office, because if she had, who knew
whether she wouldn't have taken a stick to them on account
of the unopenable windows, fraudulent windows, an arrogance of a building. Once, when she went to town to buy
fabric for a dress, Grandma Haya took one look at the prices
and threw the cloth back on the counter. "The nerve of
you," she said to the salesgirl. "The nerve of you." Then and

there she swore that she would never buy another thing until impudence passed from the world. Over her dead body would the speculators get rich. Several years before she had gone to Tel Aviv and returned in a rage; ever since, her favorite phrase of dismissal was to say, "That's from Tel Aviv." If someone brought her a box of chocolates, all becellophaned and beribboned, she would wrinkle her mouth sarcastically and ask: "Is that from Tel Aviv?" And once, when Dolly had brought her a book by some young author, she had declared after reading it: "It must be from Tel Aviv." It was common knowledge that you didn't bring Grandma Haya flowers unless you had grown them in your own garden. Flower butchers was her name for flower shops.

In the middle of the Yom Kippur War, when she had grown tired of baking cakes for the soldiers, Grandma Haya decided to step out: she had an urge to go see the Chagall stained-glass windows at Hadassah hospital. Buses either came in those days or they didn't; over half-an-hour later Dolly found her sitting on the stone bench of the bus station, and suggested that she take a taxi. "What's gotten into you, child?" Grandma Haya scolded her. Besides which, taxis were built low, you couldn't see anything out of them. Buses were built high, at least you could look out and see.

Grandma Haya no longer stepped out anymore. She was tired, tired in that quiet way that marks the end of all wanting, of even the hint of a desire. I'm not afraid to die, she told her family. I've never quarreled with my body and I don't intend to quarrel with it now.

"Come on in," she said to Dolly with a bright smile, opening the door for her. "You can help me slice string beans in the kitchen." Grandma Haya never sliced string beans the lazy way, across. She always sliced them lengthwise, her knife passing right through the little seeds in the pod. It gave them an entirely different taste.

They were seated opposite the black grandfather clock in

the kitchen. Through the short, starched muslin curtains the light half-filtered in. Dolly had no idea why she had come. If it was to bare her heart, she herself wasn't sure what there was to bare. There was an opaqueness in her that she failed to comprehend but that kept her from returning home. She was in that state of blind anticipation in which a man vaguely senses that things have come to a head, without knowing exactly what things or what head. Grandma Haya sliced string beans and talked.

"Once when Menahem, may he rest in peace, was alive, two young yeshivah students came to see him one Saturday morning. '*Doktor, kumt.*' 'Where to?' asked Menahem. 'Our rabbi has had a heart attack.' Menahem was already halfway out of the house with his doctor's case when I decided to open my mouth. 'Just how do you expect him to come with you on the Sabbath?' I asked. 'He won't be able to drive his car down your streets.' 'Then let him walk,' said the students. 'Oh no,' I said, 'oh no. My husband is a man of more than seventy, and he's not going anywhere on foot.' 'Just a minute,' said one of the students to me. 'We'd better talk things over between us.' So they went outside and whispered a bit, psss, psss, psss, and then came back in. '*Doktor, kumt!*' 'How is he going?' I asked. 'In his car,' they said. 'But they throw stones in your streets at cars traveling on the Sabbath,' I said. '*Doktor, kumt,*' they said. 'Just let him drive slowly behind us, everything will be all right.'

"So he got into his car, may he rest in peace, which by then couldn't have gone very fast anyway, neither it nor he, and drove slowly behind the two students, who walked ahead of him shouting '*Shaa! Shaa!*' to their left and to their right. When Menahem reached the police barrier blocking traffic into their quarter, the police were fast asleep, they never dreamed that anyone would try driving a car into Mea She'arim on the Sabbath. By the time they woke up, the two students had moved the barrier and Menahem had driven through. A policeman ran after them in a state of shock, shouting, 'Hey it's *shabbes!*' So what did the two students do? They turned around to him and said *Shaa!* That's how Menahem drove into Mea She'arim on the Sabbath, with the two students *shaa*'ing all the *shabbes*-criers. He examined the rabbi, gave him something to feel better, and came home. We had a good laugh over it."

"How did he get back out, with the students?"

"No, by himself."

"And what happened?"

"They stoned him of course, what do you think? Dolly, you're younger than I am, throw out this garbage and put some water in the kettle. Where is Meir?"

"Meir is in Malta. At an architects' conference."

Grandma Haya made a face.

"Why on earth Malta? What can a man expect to find in Malta? When is he coming back?"

"I don't know," Dolly confessed. "He didn't say exactly. Perhaps next week."

Grandma Haya was annoyed.

"What kind of business is that? A husband goes off to Malta-shmalta and his wife doesn't even know when he's coming back. You're an idiotic generation. I suppose you don't even know what's written in your marriage contract. In a Jewish marriage contract it says that a husband mustn't go off to the end of the earth without first asking his wife's permission. Did Meir ask your permission?"

"I gave him permission, Grandma Haya," smiled Dolly, the old, habitual darkness in her heart. "And you know he would have gone without permission anyway. That's how men are." Suddenly she found the courage to add: "Don't you think it might be better if women didn't marry men at all? Perhaps what a woman really needs is another woman."

But Grandma Haya wouldn't hear of it and flapped her hands in distress:

"What sort of nonsense is that? Really, the things you people say. A woman needs a woman, *feh*. What is this, Tel Aviv?"

Dolly made a soft, sweeping gesture with her palms, as though gathering in with great gentleness the curly head in the post office, like gathering a flower. She rose to go.

"I'll pour you your tea, Grandma Haya, and then I'll be off. Please, you needn't get up."

Grandma Haya got up anyway. In the grave, she said, is where I'll stop getting up to say goodbye to my guests. She kissed Dolly at the door with the cold lips of a person who no longer has much vital heat. "And tell Meir that I don't like this going off of his one bit. Besides which, I want him and Bilhah to close up my windows in the dining room. There's enough to do here in Jerusalem. What is he running all over the world for?"

Home, when Dolly returned to it, was warm and very clean, and smelled unmistakably of comfort and wealth. She took off her coat and sat down at the table, exhausted in advance, as though some grim and unavoidable disaster awaited her and she hadn't the strength to begin. Soon, however, God knew from where, a sharp burst of energy ran through her: now, at once, this evening, she must understand everything about herself once and for all. It was time she knew. She rummaged through the closet, took out all the albums and began feverishly looking for the few rare snapshots of herself from her refugee days. None lit the faintest spark. She could not find herself in any of them. Perhaps, she thought, if only, if only I had some picture from my childhood, from the age of four or five, perhaps then. But such a picture was not to be had anywhere on earth. It was as if Dolly had been twice-born, and her first, perhaps realer life had ended abruptly at the age of fourteen. Afterward another, post-diluvian life had begun, with its disguises and new names.

A great wave of sadistic compassion, a feeling not unlike

that of a little child who plays lovingly with a doll and a minute later punishingly tears out its hair, cast the girl from the post office up inside her again. The shame of it, thought Dolly dry-mouthedly, the wonderful shame of it. Why, I practically am in need of her. Already she was planning how the two of them would sit here, at this table, studying English together. Dolly would teach her patiently, yet sometimes not, losing her temper in a fit of erotic anger; and as the weather would be hot, and the air conditioning was out of order, the two would take off their blouses. They would wash each other in the shower. One more step and the girl would be hers, a gutterbird, scrawny and adroit.

After midnight the wave vanished as suddenly as it had come. That's the last of it, she thought tiredly, the absolute last of it. I almost made a terrible mistake. Thank God I got over it in time. The situations a person can get herself into, really. She left the night light on, took a sleeping pill, and drifted off into a deep, obtuse sleep.

At ten o'clock the next morning, without knowing a minute beforehand what she was about to do, Dolly Jacobus settled vehemently into her car, slammed the door shut with pursed lips, and drove off with a violent grinding of her gears. She parked in the usual lot, which was attended this morning by a new, unfamiliar face, and walked with quick steps in the direction of Advocate Yitzhaki's office. In her panic that she might reconsider and change her mind, she nearly ran up the steps. The lawyer's office was composed of two rooms entered from an old, peeling corridor that housed several other offices as well, in addition to a bathroom with a gigantic old key in its door and a small cubicle in which an aged, immortal-looking man sat making tea and coffee for the office workers. The older he grew, it was said, the more polished were his copper trays and the dirtier the drinking glasses borne on them.

Dolly Jacobus was still examining the nameplates on the

wall when the bathroom door swung open at the end of the corridor and the girl in the purple blouse emerged and stopped to turn the key twice behind her. She looked even tinier than she had yesterday in the post office. An ancient, wicked triumph shone in her eyes when she caught sight of Mrs. Jacobus. She stepped up to her, too concentrated a ball of impudence for one small girl.

"Would you like to come work for me?" asked Dolly Jacobus. She felt that her generally musical voice lacked all expression, was as toneless as a block of wood.

"Whaddam I gonna do fa' you?" asked the girl with a trace of scorn. "I ain't no cleaning woman. I work for a lawyer, y'know."

"I know that you do," said Mrs. Jacobus. "You're Advocate Yitzhaki's messenger girl. But wouldn't you like to get ahead in the world? I could teach you English if you'd like."

The girl stared at her blankly.

"It won't cost you a penny," said Dolly Jacobus. "You can come every day to study for an hour, an hour and a half."

The girl gave her head a skeptical shake.

"You'll be sorry y'ast." She seemed to hold the consonants and then spit them menacingly out of her mouth. Cheekily.

"Wouldn't you like to try?"

The girl looked at her askance. To do so she had to throw back her head, since Mrs. Jacobus was much taller. From the girl came the smell of a recently chewed sesame bar.

"When do you finish working here?"

"Me? At six."

"Fine. Be down near the Agron building at six. I'll be waiting for you in my car."

"Me? I can't today. I gotta date with my boy friend, see?"

So soon, so soon the degradation of it had begun. Dolly Jacobus could feel the knife that was being slowly, almost gently turned in her body. Already I am at the mercy of her whims, of her boy friend, who may or may not exist, most likely not. A terrible pity flooded her eyes. She placed a gentle hand on the girl's cheek.

"All right, little girl. Let's make it tomorrow."

The girl must have had no idea of how to respond to an innocent touch, for immediately she thrust out her hips like a streetwalker's, as though it were expected of her. Dolly Jacobus swallowed a hot lump, turned on her heels and began descending the stairs.

"Hey, missus!" called the girl after her, leaning over the balcony. "Missus! Listen, missus, it's okay. Let's make it today."

And Dolly Jacobus felt weak with happiness.

A letter was waiting for her at home from Meir, special delivery, as was his habit. She put off opening it. There were two telephone calls. A friend called to invite her and Meir to Friday night dinner, but said quickly when told that Meir was still away, "All right, then, let's make is some other time. Bye-bye, Dollinka, and send the man my best." Then Grandma Haya called, querulous, cross, and very old. Why wasn't Meir back yet? Why weren't her windows taken care of? Did they think she was going to live forever? She had completely forgotten Dolly's visit of yesterday.

Otherwise, there was nothing to do. Lust turned into a series of practical details: a meal ready in the refrigerator, plates on the table, a record that took a long time to choose, a new blouse that lay in its wrapper in the bedroom to give the girl as a gift. She had bought it in a children's store, since sizes that small were available nowhere else. Three times she went to town shopping and three times she came back. It all became so new, blind, and inevitable. Hurry, hurry.

The Agron building was very white in the dusky light. A gray haze rose from the acacia trees to mingle with the exhaust of many cars, against which the lampposts and yellow fences stood out strongly. Dolly Jacobus felt everything intensify: all shapes seemed more significant, as though—the white gleam of the stone that faced the office building, that street light over there that was trying to say a clear sentence —they were all in a code that had to be learned to be read. The cloud-dampered, haze-dimmed twilight did not surprise her: why, since last evening her world had been darkening— since well before last evening in fact—with that last, eerie glow that portends a certain disaster. I am waiting for my love, she told herself, for my poor, ugly love with her smell of sweat and synthetic violets. To support her in the style she will become accustomed to. I shall not skimp.

She waited a long time. The girl did not appear. A gang of boys on their way to Morasha passed by her car and peered apathetically inside at her. A young mother screamed at her son with practiced, despairing, almost ceremonial screams. Two foreign journalists whom she knew waved at her on their way to the press club. Suddenly, in a gust of evening breeze, the acacias began to touch one another, to talk back and forth. The city whirled the evening around inside it, rings within rings; soon it would be suppertime, soon it would be nighttime, soon there would be street lights and movies and people clustered around hot popcorn. The whirling rings slowly thickened into solid darkness. The girl had not come.

At seven o'clock, cold, beat, and aching, Dolly Jacobus pressed the accelerator and headed for home. What luck, she thought, at least she doesn't know my name and address. All I needed was to have a blackmail case on my hands, she and her boy friend together, don't get wise with us, lady, we know all about you. Or some venereal disease, who knows. How could Yitzhaki even employ such a horrible girl? Why, one ought to . . . one ought to . . .

She hurried to enter the house, which seemed to her now all Meir's: those were his clothes in the closet, his slippers on the floor. What a disgrace, really, the things she had thought of doing in it. Even the shirt from the children's store that lay on his side of the bed. Blushingly she took it and threw it in the garbage pail. I didn't do anything, Meir, she said to herself, I only thought of it—and thoughts aren't deeds, Meir, are they? She drew open the heavy curtain, which revealed the most stunning landscape on earth: the old walls of Jerusalem, the Temple Mount and Mount Zion. It's all there, she reassured herself, it's still there, all those thousands of houses dipped now in darkness as though they, as though they alone were the only true houses and deserved to have their wishes come true. She looked around her. The pictures still hung on the walls, the books hadn't vanished, her shoeless foot sunk as sensually as always into the Mashhad carpet. My God, how could I? How? The lunacy of it.

She suddenly made up her mind to call Meir. True, he had firmly, with all the authority of a rational man, warned her not to do it, so that she feared the moment of his anger and surprise—but she must hear his voice, if only to tell him about Grandma Haya's windows, or to find out the number of his return flight, just to talk. She explained to the long-distance operator that she did not know the number, but that she wanted to get the Hotel Phoenix in Valletta. Yes, Valletta, the capital of Malta, that's correct. Once again it seemed to her the most cavalier and elegant of cities. Yet it was hard for her to imagine Meir walking its streets without his car, since he had long ago turned into a centaur, part man and part automobile. It was perhaps only in bed that he sometimes still lay peeled of his layers and defenseless. Who knew what his strength was without his car in the streets of Valletta?

While waiting for the operator to call back, she prepared

herself a sandwich, which she ate sitting on the arm of the
easy chair, her bare feet crossed. Soon I will speak with Meir,
she thought, I will hear the wonder in·his voice—the same
mild wonder I always hear, as though life itself was not what
he had expected. Meir Jacobus, the architect, the man who
found it easier to talk about entrances for Zone Three of the
Jewish Quarter than about what was going on inside him.
We've drifted apart a bit lately, Meir, thought Dolly, but it
will all work out, won't it? We will talk now and it will
work out.

The sandwich was eaten. Dolly had just gone to the
kitchen to get an apple when the telephone rang. She left the
unwashed fruit by the sink and ran barefoot to the telephone.

The long-distance operator told her to wait. She heard her
talking to the operator in Valletta. Then to the desk at the
hotel. So many different voices talking so far away—Dolly
had never been very good at understanding such things. *At-
tendez un moment*, said the operator at the hotel. Then:
"Mrs. Jacobus, here's your call."

"Hello?" An unpleasant and familiar woman's voice
sounded in Dolly's ears. For a second she failed to understand: why, it was the wooden voice of Esther, ugly, gum-
chewing, wigged Esther. The secretary. Then she understood. Slowly she replaced the receiver.

The long-distance operator was persistent. She rang again.
"Your call to Valletta, Mrs. Jacobus."

"I've changed my mind," Dolly said. "Please cancel it. I've
changed my mind."

So that's how it is, said Dolly out loud in the empty apartment. That's how it's been all the time. I've really always
known. But what actors we all are.

She turned off the light and sat on the windowsill, looking
out at the broad canopy of sky and many lights. Something
fell away from her and dropped, perhaps the paths that hence-

forward would go their different ways, with cosmic speed, so that there would be no remembering even when she had still been her undivided self.

Why, one ought to, said Dolly out loud to the shadowy paintings, whose frames glittered silently in the dark room. One ought to.

Tomorrow, she thought, I'll know what one ought to do.

THE TRANSLATORS

MARY SANDBACH lives in Cambridge, England, and is married to a retired professor of classics. She has known Sweden and its writers for over fifty years. She is best known for her excellent translations of Strindberg: *Inferno, From an Occult Diary, The Cloister,* and *Getting Married.* In 1979 her translations of *Inferno* and *From an Occult Diary* were published as a Penguin Classic with an introduction by the translator. She has also translated a number of modern Swedish novels and translated or edited a good many Swedish films, including Ingmar Bergman's *Six Scenes from a Marriage* and *The Magic Flute.* In 1974 she was awarded the Swedish Order of Vasa for her services to Swedish literature.

RALPH MANHEIM, who, publishers agree, is one of the world's great translators, was born and raised in New York City. He graduated from Harvard at the age of nineteen, and then did postgraduate work in Munich and Vienna before Hitler. He has been living in Paris since 1950.

Manheim has translated in many fields: philosophy, psychology, politics, biology, history of religions, art history, and belles lettres. In recent years he has specialized in fiction and plays.

Among the books he has translated are *The Thinking Eye* by Paul Klee; *The Philosophy of Symbolic Forms* (3 volumes) by Ernst Cassirer; *Introduction to Metaphysics* by Martin Heidegger. He has translated all of Günter Grass's novels, and was co-editor with John Willett of the nine-volume Complete Dramatic Works of Bertolt Brecht. He has completed the first volume of the Selected Letters of Marcel Proust (for which he received a grant from the National Endowment for the Humanities in 1979), and is presently translating Michael Ende's *Die Unendliche Geschichte*.

Also among the authors he has translated are the Brothers Grimm (the Complete Tales), Hermann Hesse, Freud, Feuerbach, and Céline.

Ralph Manheim has won many international translation prizes, including the National Book Award (*Castle to Castle* by Céline, 1970); the Pen Club Award (*The Tin Drum* by Günter Grass, 1964); the Goethe House-Pen Translation Prize (*A Sorrow Beyond Dreams* by Peter Handke, 1976); and the Schlegel-Tieck Prize (*Dog Years* by Günter Grass, 1966; *The Resistible Rise of Arturo Ui* by Bertolt Brecht, 1977; and *The Flounder* by Günter Grass, 1979).

A Virginian, WILLIAM WEAVER drove an ambulance during World War II with the British Army in North Africa and Italy. After graduating from Princeton, he returned to Italy, where he has lived most of his life (for the past fifteen years on his farm in Tuscany). He has translated many major contemporary Italian writers, among them Silone, Morante, Bassani. He has won the National Book Award for Translation and, in England, the John Florio Prize (twice), as well as a special award from the Arts Council. He is also a music critic and a frequent lecturer and broadcaster on Italian opera. His publications include *Verdi, A Documentary Study* and *The Golden Century* (an essay on the social aspects of nineteenth-century Italian opera). At present he is on a Guggenheim fellowship, working on a biography of Eleanora Duse.

JAMES BROCKWAY, born in the United Kingdom in 1916, went to Holland after war service on fighters and bombers in Africa, India, and Burma. He published short stories, articles and poetry in London until translation took over. His translations include work by famous Dutch poets Achterberg, Lodeizen, and Campert. His fiction translations include Christopher Isherwood's *A Single Man* (into Dutch) and works by Belgian author Teirlinck, and by Dutch authors Frans Coenen, Jan Wolkers, Andreas Burnier, Heere Heeresma. In 1966 he was awarded the Dutch Martinus Nijhoff Prize for translations and services to Dutch literature. His own books include *No Summer Song* (poems, London, 1949) and (in Dutch) *Whatever Happened to the Angry Young Men?* (essays, Amsterdam, 1965). He is a regular reviewer (mainly in Dutch) of contemporary fiction, and set up a series of modern English novels in translation in Amsterdam, 1961–75.

BARBARA WRIGHT studied music in Paris, and then moved on to journalism and translation. Among the authors she has translated are Nathalie Sarraute, Jean Genet, Alain Robbe-Grillet, Roland Topor and Michel Tournier. She writes regularly on art for the *Arts Review*, and has written occasionally for the *Times Literary Supplement*.

HELEN R. LANE was born in Minneapolis in 1920, and earned advance degrees at the University of California at Los Angeles and the University of Paris in Romance Languages and Literatures. She has taught French, Spanish, and English as a Second Language and was a foreign editor at Grove Press for ten years. Since 1960 she has lived abroad, translating and writing. Among the authors whose works she has rendered into English are Jean-Paul Sartre, André Breton, Mario Vargas Llosa, and Maria Montessori. Her prize-winning translations include English versions of Octavio Paz's *Alternating Current* (National Book Award, 1973), Juan Goytisolo's *Count Julian* (American Pen Award, 1974), and *The Three Marias* (Gulbenkian Prize, 1979). An extensive interview in which Ms. Lane discusses her more than sixty translations and the problems and philosophy of her craft was recently published in *Translation Review* (Number 5, 1980). Her present home is an eighteenth-century farmhouse in Southwest France near Les Eyzies, and she is currently translating and editing a series of essays by various hands that will constitute the catalogue of a 400-piece exhibition of nineteenth- and twentieth-century art from Latin America, organized by the Museum of Modern Art in New York, which will tour Europe and the United States in 1980–81.

HILLEL HALKIN was born in 1939 in New York City and settled in Israel in 1970, where he now lives in the small town of Zichron Ya'akov with his wife and two daughters. He has been translating professionally from the Hebrew since 1961. His translations include stories and novels by such classic Hebrew authors as Agnon and Hazaz, and by such contemporary Israeli writers as Appelfeld and Amichai, in addition to works of scholarship by Gershon Scholem, Leah Goldberg and others. He himself has written numerous articles on Jewish and Israeli subjects. His first book, *Letters to An American Jewish Friend: A Zionist's Polemic*, appeared in 1977, and a second book is currently in progress.